Praise for *The Healthy Type A*™

Finally, a writer who puts it all together. Kerry Crofton understands that Candida albicans may be a root cause of fatigue, headaches, recurring infections and a weakened immune system. And she outlines for the reader a nutritional and stress treatment plan that really works."—Carolyn Dean, M.D., author of *Complementary Natural Prescriptions for Common Ailments*

* * *

"Kerry Crofton has made an absolutely fascinating contribution to the literature on health and nutrition, demonstrating that our dietary needs, especially those of Type A's, are unique. This is a wise and wonderful book that reminds us that life is not a rehearsal, but a magnificent journey to be lived and experienced completely."—Sam Graci, author of *The Power of Superfoods*

* * *

"In my practice, I see many people suffering from fatigue, recurring infections, and a range of other conditions that are related to stress and a suppressed immune system. Many doctors still treat symptoms instead of addressing causes. Kerry Crofton's excellent book will be very helpful to readers who are seeking the underlying cause, and an effective treatment plan to regain their health and energy."—James F. Balch, M.D., author of *Prescription for Nutritional Healing*

* * *

"In an easy-to-read style, Kerry Crofton deftly outlines the reasons we might lose touch with our healthy selves and—using updated techniques based on the ancient wisdom of meditation—she also gives us a smart way to come back."—Marilyn Webb, former editor-in-chief of *Psychology Today* and author of *The Good Death: The New American Search to Reshape the End of Life*

The Healthy Type A™

THE
HEALTHY
TYPE A™

Good News for Go-Getters

KERRY CROFTON, Ph.D.

MACMILLAN CANADA TORONTO

Canadian Cataloguing in Publication Data

Crofton, Kerry, 1949–
  The healthy type A : good news for go-getters

ISBN 0–7715–7554-8

1. Stress management. I. Title.
RA785.C76 1998   155.9'042   C98–930058–7

Macmillan Canada wishes to thank the Canada Council, the Ontario Ministry of Culture and Communications and the Ontario Arts Council for supporting its publishing program.

This book is available at special discounts for bulk purchases by your group or organization for sales promotions, premiums, fundraising and seminars. For details, contact: Macmillan Canada, Special Sales Department, 29 Birch Avenue, Toronto, ON M4V 1E2. Tel: 416-963-8830.

Cover design: Greg Stevenson
Interior design: Kevin Connolly
Page composition and scans: IBEX Graphic Communications Inc.

HERMAN ® is reprinted with permission of Laughingstock Licensing Inc., Ottawa, Canada

Macmillan Canada
A Division of Canada Publishing Corporation
Toronto, Ontario, Canada

1 2 3 4 5   TRI   02 01 00 99 98

Printed in Canada

To my father, Patrick D. Crofton, my guide and inspiration,

and to my mother, Anne B. Crofton, my supporter and dearest friend, my

heartfelt appreciation for your warmth, humour and unconditional love.

Acknowledgements

After the arduous journey of completing this book, I now know why authors start off thanking their families for their long-suffering support! Charles, your good-natured love and understanding are truly wonderful and, Nigel, you are a delight. My thanks to you both.

A book is a team effort. And it is quite true to say that this book would not have been written, at least not have been completed, without the unwavering dedication of my assistant, and trusted friend, Sherry Lepage. Sherry, you have helped me sort through 20 years of material and provided much-appreciated editorial expertise. My thanks to you. ·

I would also like to express my appreciation to my agents, Robert Mackwood and Perry Goldsmith of Contemporary Communications of Vancouver. Thank you both for your excellent guidance and friendship.

Nicole de Montbrun, at Macmillan Canada, is more than one could ever hope for in an editor. Your razor-sharp mind and open and understanding heart are much appreciated by this first-time author.

Alison Maclean, the publisher of Macmillan, has a brilliant and intuitive mind. You grasped the essence of the Healthy Type A Program immediately and are a great supporter. Thank you for making me part of your team.

Dee Gale, of Salt Spring Island, is a talented graphic artist, as the reader will see throughout this book. Thank you for your wonderful pictures.

My thanks also to a host of professional colleagues for their enriching contributions. To: Peter Hanson, M.D., for his kind words; Elliott Howard, M.D., for his risk factor profiles; Carolyn Dean, M.D., and James Balch, M.D., for their treatment plans; and to Thomas Budzynski, Ph.D., Joseph Campbell, Ph.D., Lisa Connoly, N.D., Barry Crofton, Lic.Ac., Abram Hoffer, M.D., James Houston, M.D., Richard Leather, M.D., Stephen Malthouse, M.D., Alex Moll, M.D., Kevin Nolan, M.D., Sheel Tangri, D.C., Glenn Timms, R.M.T., James Tucker, M.D., and Frances Wren, M.D., for their quotes.

And a special thanks to two cardiologists, whom I've never met, Meyer Friedman, M.D., and Ray Rosenman, M.D., for their pioneering work on the mind/body connection and for coining the terms Type A and Type B.

Contents

Foreword

When I first met Kerry Crofton, in Toronto more than a decade ago, she started off by telling me that she was a "healthy Type A." Of course, being a true Canadian, I assumed she was employing the national vernacular, saying she was a "healthy type, eh?" But I quickly (a speed that naturally befits this Type A) found out that Kerry was all of that and more. In speaking with her, and in hearing her presentations, I was impressed that she had it right . . . there is absolutely no point in browbeating Type A's into a totally passive behaviour pattern.

The truth is our world needs Type A's, because without them nothing much would get done. Not that Type B's aren't capable, but every successful team needs a combination of both personality types. Of course, the trick is to keep the Type A's *healthy*, otherwise they will come to an early end. Happily, Kerry has the right prescription. She keeps the good attributes of high productivity and energy and steers the Type A into strategies to stay fit both mentally and physically, so that they can enjoy a long and guilt-free life.

It was a special delight to find Kerry is as good a writer as she is a speaker. She has an excellent grasp of the character in question—no doubt due to her sharing it—and guides the way through the mine-field with clarity, humour and simplicity. Her recommendations are useful and easy to follow. This book is going to provide great help for all Type A's, and to all those who are married to or working with Type A's.

Peter G. Hanson, M.D.
author of *The Joy of Stress*
Porter Hospital, Denver, Colorado

Introduction

We have become a society plagued with "time sickness." Caught up in the stress of running from work, to home, to recreation, or to other responsibilities, no one seems to have the time to do the important things. Anxious about the future, regretful of the past, we miss the hidden fullness of each moment.

Stephan Rechtschaffen, M.D.
Time Shifting: A Guide to Creating More Time to Enjoy Your Life

If you're the kind of go-getter who will benefit from this book, you're probably going to skip this part. Introductions—and instructions—are meant for those slower-paced types.

You've too much to do. You've no time. No patience?

So, if you're in the hurry-up mode, jump ahead. But you might take a quick glance at the following questionnaire, as taking stock of your stress is the first step in becoming a healthy go-getter.

Signs of Stress

If you experience a sign and it occurs **often, score 2**, if it occurs **occasionally, score 1**. If it seldom occurs or is well under control, leave it blank.

	Often	Occasionally
On-the-spot signs (cues) (not due to exercise):	____	____
1. Rapid heartbeat	____	____
2. Shallow or rapid breathing	____	____
3. Holding, or trouble getting, your breath	____	____
4. Sweaty palms	____	____
5. Cool hands	____	____
6. Feeling tense, difficulty sitting still	____	____
7. Tight muscles	____	____
8. Clenched jaw	____	____
9. Finger- or foot-tapping	____	____
10. Nail biting	____	____
11. Feeling hot and flushed	____	____
12. Stuttering	____	____
13. Dry mouth	____	____
14. Tightness in throat	____	____
15. Knots in the stomach, feeling of racing inside	____	____
16. Upset stomach	____	____

Other signs		
17. Difficulty concentrating	____	____
18. Trouble making decisions	____	____
19. Forgetfulness	____	____
20. Mind races	____	____
21. Mind goes blank	____	____
22. Short fuse	____	____
23. Can't stop worrying	____	____
24. Not sleeping well	____	____
25. Compulsive eating or loss of appetite	____	____
26. Increased smoking or alcohol use	____	____
27. Use of tranquillizers, sleeping pills	____	____
28. Fatigue	____	____
29. Loss of humour	____	____
30. Negative or overly critical	____	____
31. Loss of interest in sex and/or intimacy	____	____
32. Avoiding being alone or around others	____	____
33. Crying easily or uncontrollably	____	____
34. Feeling flat, apathetic	____	____

Add these columns to get your total score   ____   +   ____

0–10 Reasonable   11–20 High   21–30 Very High   31–40 Extreme   41+ Extreme Plus

If you scored in the higher ranges, you're too stressed too often. Your system is crying out for balance—for some down time. Your stamina and even your life are at risk. Your mate has been telling you this? Your doctor? Your own body?

If you scored in the middle, your health may still be okay, but you may be plagued by fatigue and many other stress symptoms. This book will help you to gain more energy and balance, and prevent more serious problems.

If you scored in the lower ranges, skim through the first section of this book and dig in when you get to the behavioural strategies in Step 8, "Transform Your Critic into a Coach." Then in Step 9, "Balance Your Mind, Body and Spirit," you'll learn how to tame your mind and reconnect with the natural energies within and around you.

The Plate Game

If you remember watching "The Ed Sullivan Show," you might recall a juggler similar to the one depicted above. His props included a stack of dinner plates and a pile of thin sticks. He would pick up a plate and twirl it on one of the sticks. Then he would start another, then another, and another, until he had a whole line of plates spinning. Everyone applauded.

When the first plate began to totter, he would run to it and spin its stick again; then the fourth would begin to wobble, and he would run to it. Soon, he was racing madly back and forth among the plates, trying to keep them all spinning. Sound familiar?

In many ways, our lives have become like the plate game: meeting deadlines at work, tackling difficulties at home, getting gas in the car and putting meals on the table. Like the juggler, we have to scramble from one task to the other, just to keep the plates—our projects—going. We run flat out all day. No time to rest. No time to recharge. No time to enjoy our lives. This is stress!

Tuning in

Most of us tune into the build-up of stress rather late in the game. In a recent Relax/Recharge seminar, I asked a gathering of business people, "How do you know when you're too stressed?" A person at the back of the room called out brightly, "That's easy. I can tell right away. I get chest pains!" The group couldn't help laughing. Gently, I suggested that it would be helpful to tune in *before* the chest pains.

The key to taking charge of stress is to wake up and recognize your early warning stress cue and then to gear down; I'm going to show you how to do this in Step 3. A healthy Type A knows how to minimize the wear and tear of a go-getter style and a high-pressure life: with balance and flexibility, and emphasis on being, as well as doing.

I've spent 20 years working with thousands of people who scramble to keep their plates spinning. Many felt they were doing more and enjoying it less. They were longing for balance.

Among the comments were these:

I'm fried. My life is leading me. All my time and energy go into keeping the whole thing going. I'm a bear at work, and no better at home.

And the worst part is I'm not having any fun. It's affecting my marriage, my children, my job. Recently, I read your column about burn-out, as I was flaked out on the couch. Boy, did it hit home.

Is my life just going to be more of this? Getting older, greyer and more exhausted? Even making money isn't so much of a thrill any more. What I'd like more than anything is to feel content. You know, the old thing about peace of mind. My mind is buzzing so fast. I can't stay focused. And I have a heck of a time getting to sleep.

We don't have to live like this. Let me show you how to take better care of yourself sooner, reconnect with your heart and with others, and find greater meaning.

A Question of Balance

More than 20 years ago, two American cardiologists, in California, noticed two distinct behaviour patterns among their patients. Some patients were low key and reserved; most, however, were high-energy, impatient, easily angered individuals who suffered from a sense of urgency.

In their best seller *Type A Behavior and Your Heart*, Meyer Friedman, M.D., and Ray Rosenman, M.D., labelled the low-key ones "Type B's" and the others "Type A's," terms that had nothing to do with blood types. These doctors had lots to say about Type A personalities, calling them "overly competitive" and "hostile" and deeming this behaviour "coronary prone."

If that were not enough, they went on to prescribe that Type A's "abolish this defect with an anti-Type A program to re-engineer themselves into Type B's—passive people who prefer to remain silent and listen while others talk."

I should mention, in their defence, these doctors have since updated their views. Yet, the relationship between Type A and heart disease is still being debated; the current thinking is that the hostility factor part of the Type A behaviour pattern is responsible for the coronary risk.

In 1978, a few years after Drs. Friedman and Rosenman's book came out, I was directing a stress management program at a cardiac clinic. Virtually all of the patients were Type A's. Did they consider their strong-willed style a defect? Never!

Among them was Frank, the heavy-set owner of a large construction company who declared, "It was my Type A drive that built up my business. This so-called defect has served me well."

He pounded the table with his fist and protested, "Why, I wouldn't be here today if it weren't for my Type A style." A friend leaned over and said quietly, "You're in a coronary clinic, Frank. I think that's what they're talking about."

Frank joined in the laughter. Most members of the group concurred that some of their behaviour may have been a factor in their heart attacks. None of them, however, agreed with the premise in that book. "Become a Type B?" another bellowed. "The last thing I want is to be one of those plodders. They drive too slowly. Talk too slowly. Take forever to get anything done."

Eventually, I realized that everyone has some Type A or Type B behaviours but that each of us has a basic style: a person is either mostly a dynamic doer or mostly a low-key watcher. And this is a fundamental energy with which we are born, not just a behaviour that we learn.

There are lots of times when we powerhouse doers flake out on the couch and don't want to do anything. When this happens, we are not Type B; we're pooped-out A's who want a break. And when low-key watchers take a risk and speak out, they've not become Type A's; they're emboldened B's who've decided to be heard.

Human beings are wonderfully complex creatures who cannot be pigeon-holed. The question is this: what is our fundamental style? Are we mostly a jump-in head-first doer, or are we cautious watchers? Once we've determined what type we are, transforming and balancing our fundamental energy is the key to becoming healthier and happier A's or B's.

Another vital aspect of the program set out in this book is how we recognize when our fuel is running low and how to recharge. In my clinical practice, I have worked with many men and women suffering from burnout. I longed to have an opportunity to reach them before this stage—this is what has inspired me to write this book.

Marie, a successful entrepreneur, strode into my office telling me about the pressure in her life. "I'm so wrung out all the time. I'm at cross purposes with my staff half the time. A friend told me she was worried about me and asked if I was happy. 'Happy,' I thought. 'What's that?' I'm just struggling to get out of bed each morning."

We worked together for four months. It was a lesson in flexibility for me because Marie often cancelled her appointments at the last minute, saying, "I'm just swamped. Can't get away."

But we hung in there with each other. And by the third month she turned up each week for her appointment looking better and better. "I'm still not sure what happiness means to me. But I have much more energy.

I'm sleeping much better. I'm able to fend off infections faster. I'm getting along better with others, and I know what you mean by enjoying the moment. When I think of how much I have missed over these years . . ."

The anecdotes I tell reflect my own quest to find greater energy, greater balance and greater meaning in life. To connect with the natural energies that pervade this world. The program set out here is the one I've been presenting in my counselling practice and my workshops with tens of thousands of people in every province of Canada. It's based on my professional training and on my own personal journey.

I know in my heart that we go-getter A's have so much untapped potential—so much capacity to be more fulfilled, to have more nurturing relationships, to make a significant contribution.

We have many admirable traits—one is we want more. More out of ourselves, out of others and out of life. So let's do it. But let's do it in a skillful way. Rather than spinning our wheels while we're spinning all those plates, let's learn to pace ourselves.

The Elevator Game

I was in a high-rise office tower recently and was watching how irritated and revved-up people were, having to wait the agonizing *two* minutes to get to their floor. Every time someone got out, there was a rush to pound the Door Close button, to speed up that painful process of letting someone out when what you want is to get to *your* floor.

I could see the steam billowing out of their ears and their taut faces flush with heat. What I couldn't see was the adrenalin raging through their bloodstream and flooding every cell in the body.

As you'll see, being all geared up with nowhere to go is harmful, so to save humanity, I've developed the executive Busy Box* for the elevator. Now you will have buttons to push and dials to dial. This won't accomplish anything, but that's okay; at least you'll be busy.

Why Bother?

Unhealthy Type A's are too stressed, too often. This can lead to a series of health problems, and the numbers are daunting. Of all visits to the doctor's office, 70 to 80 percent are stress related. If you don't believe this, ask a doctor.

Taking charge of the stress in our lives is the basis for becoming a healthy Type A.

Many other factors besides stress can affect health: family history, smoking, alcohol abuse, lack of exercise, how often you have fries and gravy. All these conditions contribute to the physical and mental wear and tear of high-pressure or high-anxiety lives. This brings the blood pressure up, tightens muscles, hampers digestion and, over time, drains energy, reduces production of sex hormones and suppresses the immune system.

Why I Wrote This Book

We Type A's have had a lot of bad press. It is true that many of us grind ourselves into the ground. But there are other drawbacks to ignoring the need

*(a Hasbro trademark)

for balance. The more high-energy we are, the more challenging it is for us to find peace of mind and develop a connection with others. We "come on too strong," they complain. We're "too definite," "too controlling," "too forceful." We don't listen. "Yes, but . . ."

It is unfair. We're often chastised by the very people who benefit from our drive and determination. I have learned, however, to listen to the other point of view and use that feedback to fertilize the field of growth, to breathe and let go and let others "fumble" their way along. It's so agonizing because I could do it so much quicker! But speed is not always the best objective.

I've learned to slow down and soften my edges, and be more open. Yes, I can still tear around town with the best of them; I haven't lost my good Type A zest. I have, however, let go of unrealistic expectations and striving to prove myself. This has freed up a lot of energy. Opportunities to be playful, to savour the moment, abound. I wrote this book to share this journey with you.

The Program

People tell me this program has changed their lives. Now they have the tools to take charge, not by tightening their grip, but by letting go. And they know how to tune in to the build-up of stress, and gear down without relying on scotch, chocolate, cigarettes or valium. The Healthy Type A Program starts off with the basics: how to balance our style, pace ourselves, and cool down and soothe the system. And there's lifestyle stuff, such as cutting back on the stress-producing drug caffeine and using power foods to boost the immune system for greater stamina and to prevent burn-out.

The journey continues with training the mind, stabilizing the emotions and synchronizing the body and mind so that our inner energy—called *chi*—flows smoothly.

We healthy Type A's don't burn out because we're aware when we're running low on fuel, and we know how to recharge. We also know how to connect with the limitless source of *chi* and the natural energies of the world around us.

The goal is awareness and more skillful action—to respond appropriately in a given situation. When it's best to be assertive, we do that with gentleness; when it's best to let go, we do that with grace. And we know how to have a genuinely good time.

This program is about becoming more fully who we are. More fully alive. There is so much more to living than . . .

Frank & Ernest reprinted by permission of Newspaper Enterprise Association Inc.

Notes to Myself

If you feel inspired, jot down some thoughts that come to you about your life, your style, your aspirations . . . or skip ahead. Doodle in the margins. Scribble down your brainwaves here and there. Let your creative A run wild. This is your book. This is your journey.

Take Stock of Your Style

You possess Type A behavior pattern if, on meeting another severely afflicted Type A person, instead of feeling compassion for his affliction you find yourself compelled to challenge him...Luckily, the behavior pattern of most Type A persons is not crippled beyond repair. Most still retain, to some extent, a sense of humor.

Meyer Friedman, M.D., and Ray Rosenman, M.D.
Type A Behavior and Your Heart

It's a bright summer day and Mr. and Mrs. Type A are flopped in their lounge chairs. Ahhhh...it feels good to sit down with a steaming cup of coffee and the weekend paper. It's been a crazy week for both of them. By the weekend they're ready to collapse.

But the seats on their chairs barely have time to get warm before Mr. A notices the hedge needs trimming. He approaches this job the same way as he does everything else: he leaps into action and attacks it. He snips away furiously at one side, then the other. When he's finished, the hedge is trimmed, all right—and quite a bit smaller too.

Now, on to the next thing. With Mr. A, it's always on to the next thing; there's no gap between projects to savour the results, no pause to rest. By the end of the morning, he is worn out and wonders how his neighbours could extol the delights of gardening.

Mrs. A, in turn, attacks the flower bed. Undaunted by the fact that she doesn't really know what she's doing, she yanks out weeds (are those weeds?) and thrusts plants into the ground. Mrs. A is a dedicated consumer and likes to buy gardening books, but she doesn't have the patience to actually read them. "Read that gardening book? Don't be ridiculous. You'll never get anything accomplished if you sit around reading instructions."

Their next-door neighbours, Mr. and Mrs. B, are also weekend gardeners, but in a different way. Trimming the hedge, like all other projects, is carefully thought out. First, Mr. B sits back and studies the hedge, from every angle. (He has a sign in his workshop that reads, Think Twice, Cut Once.) Wouldn't want to make any mistakes. No need to rush.

As for Mrs. B, those weeds aren't going anywhere and can easily wait until next weekend. Later, she may putter about, but there's no hurry. She loves to lounge.

Which of the above scenarios sounds like your usual style of getting things done? Are you the jump-in type who rushes at everything? Or the cautious kind who approaches projects tentatively?

The first step or challenge to becoming a healthy Type A is to see ourselves clearly: are we mostly a Type A or mostly a Type B? In my seminars, I ask the participants to join the A or the B discussion group. (One fellow couldn't make up his mind. He was standing in the centre of the room. A co-worker called out, "Bob, if you can't decide, you must be a B. Come over here.")

I also ask the groups to begin by selecting a moderator to take notes. At a recent program, after more than half of the time for the exercise had passed, I stopped in on the Type A group and asked how things were going. "Great," one woman shot back, "we're down to the last three finalists for the moderator."

People can have both A and B traits. Even an exact fifty-fifty mix. But most people have more of one energy than the other.

There's also a challenging swirl of healthy and unhealthy traits. Balance within one's own style—A or B—is healthy. Extremes are unhealthy. And when we're in an unbalanced mode, daily life can be fraught with Type A "tortures":

Type A Torture # 1—Slow Lines

The line at your bank is barely moving. To calm your restlessness and to give yourself the illusion you're not wasting time, you strategize: "Let's see, that teller looks efficient. I want to deal with her, not that one over there, who's being trained."

All of this is futile, of course, as you will have to go to the next available teller. And, sure enough, eventually you draw the young trainee. You brace for this assault on your dwindling patience. "Surely he's not old enough to be out of school?" you mutter angrily, knowing this comment is yet another sign you're growing older.

It's painful to watch the trainee's hesitating movements. You feel the spring inside you coiling tighter and tighter. He is trying to figure out the complicated transactions you keep thrusting at him. You're fighting the impulse to reach over the counter, grab your cheques and do the job yourself. (At any checkout counter, you have a tendency to hurl your purchases into the bag, grab the receipt out of the bewildered cashier's hand, stuff your change into your wallet and get on to the next task.)

In these situations, if you could see through the fog of your impatience, you would notice your jaw is locked, with a viselike grip, your neck and shoulder muscles are tensed rock hard and your stomach is beginning to burn. Your body is ready for battle. This is the unhealthy kind of stress.

How is it that other people "trapped" in the line manage to keep their cool?

Heavily medicated? No. There is another possibility: not everyone has a high-voltage nervous system. Or a strong sense of urgency. Or inner dictums that insist on always being on-the-go; always being on time. Some people take things as they come.

Type A's hate waiting for anything or anyone. After all, waiting is like committing that heinous crime: wasting time. And because unhealthy A's are always trying to squeeze too many things into too little time, they're always running behind schedule, in a panic. Give them a ten-minute gap and they'll do their best to jam 20 minutes worth of tasks into it.

Type A Torture #2—Slow Machines
And then there are the machines—supposedly here to ease our way—that become instead a source of frustration. They're out to foil us. It's agonizing being kept on hold on the phone. Waiting for the light to change. Waiting for the toast to pop up. Waiting for the microwave to reheat our dinner. And

high on many lists are those machines in public washrooms for drying hands. When I showed the picture above to one group, a woman confessed, "I don't bother. I just give my wet hands a flick, then fluff my hair with them as I walk out of the washroom!"

For some more patient and thorough Type B's, it is a different story.

"What's the rush?" she wonders as she methodically dries off each hand. Her friend is shouting from the doorway, "Hurry up!"

"Just a minute. There is a wet spot here on one side of my finger..."

(As you know, many B's hate being rushed. And as A's usually hate waiting, it's amazing to think that we try to work together. Live together. And go places together.)

After this discussion, I remember asking one seminar group, "What happens in the men's washroom?" A fellow called out, "No problem. We don't bother to wash *our* hands!"

Type A Torture #3—Business Travel

The landing gear has just been deployed, and the A's are ready to go, coats on and briefcases in hand; they're waiting to sprint down the aisle that too soon will be clogged with other passengers. But the A has to keep ahead of the next guy and has to be first out of the plane, first out of the airport—and first at just about everything else. Obsessive competitiveness in unhealthy Type A's can be a constant source of stress for them—and others. It's a ruthless battle, with no room for much heart or much conscience.

Minor challenges become major turf wars, leading to conflict with co-workers or loved ones. Potential friends and allies become opponents.

Paranoia can replace camaraderie. There's nothing like constantly fighting to win at everything to elicit the fight-or-flight mode. The unhealthy Type A slogan is "I work to win. I play to win. And I win at all costs."

Type A Torture # 4—Enforced Inactivity

You know you're an unhealthy Type A when you've got ten years of holiday time saved up. (How could you take a holiday? They can't get by without you.)

In a cardiac clinic, I worked with a couple who finally went on vacation, after ten years of marriage, after the husband's heart attack. On a secluded tropical isle, she became worried that her husband was going to have another heart attack. He was racing up and down the beach, trying to beat the kids at races and build the biggest sandcastle. Then he made a deal to buy land for a condo development. Relaxation? What's that?

"For heaven's sake, Ogden, it's vacation time.
Must you make your little lists even on vacation?"

Type A Torture # 5—Being Told You're a Work Addict

One woman I counselled told me the main problem with her marriage was that her husband was more in love with work than he was with her. She called him a work addict.

Hurt by the label, he flatly denied this obsession. "That's not true. And you're part of the reason I have to work so hard. And the kids. And the mortgage."

She replied, "Yes. That's true, and I appreciate you and how hard you work. But I really wish you would pace yourself and take some time to be with us. We don't have a life any more. Remember what happened the other night when I called out to you that it was late and I wanted you to come to bed? You arrived with an armload of files and then set them out all over the bed!"

Many overloaded people have "plates" that they can't allow to totter and smash. (It's difficult to downsize one's life without giving up our jobs or our children.) Mounting bills spur us on. High levels of adrenalin add momentum. High levels of caffeine propel the hectic pace. Even if we want to slow down, it's difficult.

The speedier we are, the more we need to slow down and the less likely we are to do it.

The Plate Game in Overload

But for some people, working hard is a drug. The energy surge of adrenalin is thrilling and addictive. They love the buzz. They are addicted to the buzz. They work long hours whether they need to or not. They take work on holidays—if they take holidays. They're driven. By what? Perhaps, by an old longing to please ambitious parents or to prove their worth to the world. Perhaps excessive work is a means of avoidance.

Whatever the cause, for work addicts, identity is inextricably linked to accomplishment. Their level of self-importance rises with each additional plate they spin.

Sadly, leading a frantic life is seen, by some, as an indication of status. Eventually, most crash under the weight of this largely self-imposed load.

Frank & Ernest reprinted by permission of Newspaper Enterprise Association Inc.

We can joke about workaholics, but this is a serious health hazard and social issue. The Japanese have a term for it: *karoshi* means death by over-work. It is a recognized syndrome and the fate of many workaholics. According to a 1997 United Nations report, the average Japanese takes off a mere nine days of holidays a year.

But it's not just some hard-driving Asian countries that suffer from an out-of-whack work ethic. Although we take more holiday time than the Japanese, researchers at Carleton University found that the typical Canadian employee works an average of 45 to 50 hours a week. And Statistics Canada reports that one in three of us feels continually stressed for time.

Our culture and some of our companies don't help. One overworked government employee complained that to get anywhere in his department, "You have to work weekends. The deputy minister is there all weekend and you have to show your face." (Wonder if anyone ever checked that out with the deputy. Maybe she was trying to get work off her desk when there was no one else around?)

With all the downsizing going on in companies, those of us who are fortunate enough to have jobs are putting in many extra hours. And the fear of winding up on the unemployment rolls makes it hard for people to demand more manageable conditions.

Old-style, soulless organizations, feeling the economic pinch, drive their people to do more with less. Progressive organizations—and there aren't enough of these—recognize that running their people into the ground actually leads to lower productivity, higher costs in stress leave and staff turnover.

The American Management Association recently surveyed a number of companies to see whether downsizing had any effect on the number of disability claims filed by employees. The result: 70 percent of the companies that had cut jobs and restructured their organizations reported a substantial increase in disability claims for psychiatric or psychological problems, cardiovascular conditions, chronic fatigue, back injuries, repetitive strain injuries and many other reasons.

Many work addicts simply love what they do, are very good at it and are happy when they are busy. Fair enough. But if they're not taking time to refuel, eventually they'll burn out.

It Doesn't Have to Be This Way

Remember the serenity prayer? We can learn to change what we can, accept what we cannot and have the wisdom to know the difference. Take a look at the pressure that comes from outside of you and that comes from inside. Then, take a closer look at where some of that inner pressure may come from.

You can be hard working and have a life. You can be high-energy and be at ease. You can get ahead in your career without trying to beat everyone else down.

The essence of that Type A energy can be transformed into more positive expressions that are energetic, confident, accomplished, visionary, dynamic. You can be a leader and a team player. You can get things done and enjoy them. You can focus on what is at hand, rather than on what is coming up next. It's a question of balance, flexibility and appropriateness, and these are things you'll learn with this program.

First, take a moment to fill out the quiz on the following page to take stock of your style. Circle the words or phrases that best describe you. A portrait develops as you go across.

The key to transforming your style is to develop greater balance, flexibility and appropriateness. You see what action is required and you take it: sometimes you need to be dominant, so you rouse your strength; sometimes dominance is an obstacle, so you rouse your gentleness. This is called "skillful means."

Problems can arise if you're high or low across the board. An extreme high or low calls for balance, *not* another opportunity to beat yourself up. You'll gain genuine insight if you can avoid self-blaming.

These imbalances are workable. For example, if you realize that you are too quick to take control, be more aware of this as you do it. See the effect. See the potential. You can learn to pause or step back and let others participate at their pace. You can tame and transform your energy and become an inspiring leader.

Reflect, for a moment: when your internal pressure cooker heats up, do you go to the extreme end on the scale? For example, when overly stressed, you may bite off someone's head for foolishly entering your space. If you do, this means that in a tough situation when your family or your team needs you, you're no help.

Is your style fluid or fixed? You're talking to the contractor who's behind schedule. You've got to be forceful, right? But do you need to blow her right out of the water? And do you need to dump that fury on the next unsuspecting person who pokes his head into your office?

Another off-balance trap is the impatient speech patterns of the fast-talking Type A's. "Yep. Uh huh. Got it." You slam down the receiver while the other person is still talking. Well, *you've* finished talking, even if he hasn't.

Are You Mostly Type A or Type B?

	Anger, confrontation	Ambition	Time	Taking charge	Confidence	Approach to change, new things
Unhealthy A	Hostile, hot reactor	Driven, fiercely competitive	Ruled by tyranny of time	Aggressive, domineering	Arrogant	Reckless
	Easily angered	Very ambitious	Feel urgency	Forceful	Self-promoting	Risk-taker
Healthy A	Slow to anger	Dynamic, no need to prove yourself	Conscious of time but not ruled by it	High-energy and allowing	Radiate confidence	Adventurous
Healthy B	Gentle, even-tempered	Calm, no need to prove yourself	Conscious of time but not ruled by it	Low-key and allowing	Quietly confident	Inquisitive
Unhealthy B	Shy away from confrontation	Laid back	Lose track of time easily	Hesitant	Unsure, hold back	Cautious
	Fear confrontation	Apathetic, lack drive	Oblivious to time	Passive	Low self-esteem, fear taking a stand	Fear change

You usually jump in and finish the sentence of those tiresome slow talkers. If you're not going to finish it, I'll finish it for you. This may rush things along so you shave off a few more precious seconds, but what about your communication with that person?

You can choose how to react. When you make a presentation, I want you to rev up your dynamic energy and speak with passion. Go get 'em.

When your loved one tells you about the day's details, settle down and be quiet. Firing off your expert solutions is not necessary. Just listen. Yes, of course A's can do that. (Think how many relationships would be healed if we could listen without judging or providing advice or solutions. How do you do that? Just listen with an open heart.)

You can be a forceful talker and a sensitive listener. How? By learning to balance your energy, soften your edges and sharpen your awareness.

How Did We Get Like This?

There's lots of stuff to consider on that graph we've just looked at. Basically, though, it boils down to this: we A's were born with our brains and nervous systems wired in a particular way, and then we were conditioned.

What We Brought with Us

At a meeting some time ago, a group of colleagues was debating the relative and absolute qualities of Types A and B, and of introversion and extroversion. Our host, a respected cardiologist, asserted that these traits were all conditioned, without a basis in physiology. As he was expounding, his toddler twins came to the doorway. One leaped into the centre of the gathering, greeting us with smiles, and twirled around, bounding from one empty chair to another. Meanwhile, her sister stood still, in the doorway, with her head slightly bowed, and watched this performance, never uttering a word. I couldn't resist—I leaned over and asked why he was conditioning his young daughters to be so distinctly different.

We A's were born with a quicker-to-react nervous system. A study done some years ago demonstrated a distinct difference in reactivity in infants: some were much quicker to respond to stimuli, more "hyperactive," more willing to engage with people. This was before much conditioning had occurred.

The Two Sides of the Brain

All these labels—A and B, introvert and extrovert—are indicative of the wonderful complexity of who we are. Another factor is called "brain lateralization"—how the left and right sides of the brain work differently, and how this polarity affects us.

To simplify a complex subject, the two halves of our brain are joined together with a little bridge called the "corpus collosum." In 1981, Dr. Roger Sperry was awarded the Nobel prize for his split-brain studies. He discovered each side has its specialties: our intellectual professor lives in the left brain and works like a computer, and our creative artist lives in the right and works more like a kaleidoscope.

The classic British stiff upper lip is accomplished by the professor of the left repressing the artist of the right.

If the left brain is damaged by a stroke, a patient tends to become morose and emotionally depressed—functions that reside in the right brain. If the right brain is damaged, the patient relies more on the left and is unemotional and detached.

In another split-brain study involving epileptics, one researcher had the bright idea of cutting the bridge between the two hemispheres. This stopped the seizures. However, the procedures were stopped when it became clear that severing the connections in the brain created some very bizarre behaviour: one of the subjects reached out with one hand for a piece of pie while the other hand reached out and slapped it. (Behaviour all too familiar to dieters.)

Being judgemental and critical is the result of an overly dominant left hemisphere. Too much right hemisphere can make us wild and irresponsible. We need to be creative, but we also need to balance our cheque-books. (Salvador Dali often used his cheques as bookmarks.)

Left-brained dominant types may control with logic—hot and aggressive or cool and detached. Well-developed analytical powers may keep feelings—and others—at bay. Intimacy, spontaneity, emotional risks and commitment become a threat. The reasoning mind can become a protective cocoon.

With this one-sided strength, the emotional side feels weaker, less up to being called upon in a crunch. And with so little "air time," it's less willing to be exposed. The emotional underbelly is kept hidden. A life like this is safe but lonely; it lacks depth and passion.

The aim is to balance our analytical ability with our creative ability, and have the flexibility to access one or the other appropriately. This is called "whole brain thinking" and is an essential step in becoming a healthy Type A.

Continuing on the path of awareness, reflect on the past with non-judgemental eyes.

How Balanced Is Your Brain?

The actual functioning of your brain is more complex, more holistic than this simple, dualistic picture, and not all brains work the same way. However, to get a sense of your tendencies, circle the phrases that best describe you most of the time.

Left-Brain Tendencies	Right-Brain Tendencies
Analytical	Creative
Mathematical	Artistic
Like numbers, details	Rely on intuition
Logical	Lead from your heart
Quick to criticize	Emotional
Time conscious	Holistic
Goal oriented	Spontaneous
Rely on intellect	Like things to be carefree
Lead from your mind	Playful
Like things ordered	Sensuous, luxuriate in the moment
Linear	Tuned in to your senses
Verbal	Like colours
Rational	Allowing
Can appear chilly to others	Nonverbal
Like things well planned	Tactile
Fear intimacy, letting go	Physical
Made uncomfortable by emotional displays	Enjoy the journey, not so focused on the goal
Controlling	Rely on feelings
Can be rigid with fixed beliefs	Like warmth, intimacy
Maintain that rules should be followed	Love to snuggle
Masculine – Yang	Feminine – Yin
Scientific "western" thought	Mystical "eastern" thought

What We Learned

Here, I want to show you one of my baby pictures.

**"SLOW DOWN ... WATCH THAT PUSSY CAT ...
TURN RIGHT HERE."**

Reprinted by permission of Laughingstock Licensing Inc.

Inborn energies manifest themselves as sane or neurotic behaviours partly as a result of how we are punished and rewarded. The karma we brought into this life factors in there somewhere, but much depends on our environment. Ponder, for a moment, what happens when a dynamic, left-hemisphere-dominant person is born into a family in which risk taking and academic pursuits are discouraged.

What happens when a low-key, creative person is born into an ambitious family in which artistic endeavours are scorned and scholastic and monetary achievements highly valued?

Our out-of-kilter society encourages left-brain achievements and characteristics and holds less store by right-brain creativity. There is more emphasis on doing. Less on being. This imbalance in our culture and in ourselves can create a feeling of hollowness and dissatisfaction. We are not being true to our genuine nature, not doing the job we really want to do, or living the lives we really want to live. We're disconnected from our own hearts, and we long for more passion, meaning and colour. Our lives are jam-packed, but we feel empty inside.

Growing up as a "misfit" can make it difficult to find out who you really are. The wholeness of your genuine nature lies—unaltered—beneath the musty weight of unrealistic expectations.

It's useful to sort out this jumble of inherent sane and acquired neurotic traits. A workshop participant, confused by all my charts—imagine that!—remarked, "Everyone thinks I'm a Type A, but I'm not aggressively competitive." You don't have to have *all* the traits of a Type A to be a Type A.

Type A's are spirited racehorses and delight in winning a race. That does not mean being aggressively competitive is our basic nature. At heart, we like to frolic in the fields and kick up our heels. That is an expression of our high spirits, not neuroses. Compulsions and other habitual patterns are learned and can be cut through.

© 1981 Los Angeles Times Syndicate

"Yes, I might be more comfortable in my pyjamas, but in the morning I intend to hit the ground running"

Reprinted by permission L.A. Times Syndicate.

The boy in this cartoon is the president of the Grade 3 Junior Achievers. He was born with a quick-to-react nervous system, and then values, expectations and goals were instilled in him. As an adult, he will still hear the echo of his mother's voice, "Don't just sit there, do something. You know idle hands are the devil's workshop."

Inner Battle Set by Early Lessons

Kim is a scientist who came to this country several years ago. Like most immigrants, she's striving for success in her new country. She is single-minded in her drive and determination. She was brought up this way. (Her doctor referred her to me for stress-related headaches.)

Kim has a teenage son, Bill. He is very bright but spends most of his time hanging out with his friends, listening to music and watching television. This is hard for Kim to accept. She is anxious about her son's future and doesn't understand his lack of ambition.

"How do you expect to get anywhere in life if you're always going to the mall with your friends?" she complains. "You should be studying; you have to get top marks to get into university."

Bill doesn't respond. He turns and walks out the door with his skateboard tucked under his arm. Kim, angry, frustrated and worried, feels another headache coming on.

From the day we are born, we are being shaped. With the best of intentions, our parents imprint us with messages of what is "good" and what is "bad." Much of this is very useful, like when to say "please" and "thank you" and how to cross a busy street.

There are, however, other messages, also given with the best intentions, which are mixed blessings. Mummy and Daddy want all the best for us. So they teach us to "be the best." This is often interpreted by us as "I am worthy when I win." And we may assume the opposite follows: "When I am not winning, I am not worthy."

We praise good behaviour and punish failure. And our children, who long for approval, either comply like Kim or rebel like Bill.

Kim feels guilty when she takes time for herself. She no longer needs the actual voice of her parents prodding her to excel; the tape is deeply imbedded in her brain.

This inner program is something she could have carried, unconsciously, her whole life. So, if I'd simply counselled her about taking things easier, this would have gone against her unconscious code, and no long-term progress would have occurred. It is essential to address this conditioning before attempting to reduce stress. Attitude is the first place to focus, not action.

Kim was also inculcated with an unquestioning respect for her parents. Their word was law. But her son won't even stay and listen to her, and this sends waves of distressing emotion to flood her mind. Despite all her outer success, she feels she has failed miserably as a parent and in life.

Although she comes across as serious and logical, underneath Kim's well-groomed exterior lies a heart with more passion for life than she could ever imagine. As Kim would soon discover, if she were to put brush to paper, a delicate touch would emerge with inspiring beauty. So much creativity and tenderness hide beneath the surface.

Kim is an example of the difference between the person we really are and the person we are made to be.

Sadly, she has lost the ability to really enjoy anything, even the fruits of her hard work. Accolades from her colleagues feel hollow because she was taught to avoid pride, and she does not feel worthy of this praise. And the speediness of her mind zooms her attention on to the next thing she's doing. It's difficult to savour the moment, when you're not present.

Kim doesn't really enjoy time away from her work because she feels guilty. She often feels so tense that she paces around her house and yard looking for more projects to tackle. When she slows down, she not only feels guilty but comes dangerously close to feeling the emptiness of her life. So the speed of the plate game actually serves her quite well.

Like many hard-working go-getters, Kim is lonely. Achieving an open, loving relationship is not part of her script. Intimacy is hard for her. She feels out of control.

The realtor, Aaron, who sold her the townhouse, seemed to be particularly attentive even after the sale. She did not understand why until he asked her out for dinner.

Aaron, also a Type A, has taken the term *go-getter* to dizzying heights. The sign outside his office and his business card proudly proclaim, I Never Sleep!

Aaron's parents worked hard their whole lives and wanted so much for their son. From an early age they encouraged him to excel. And he did. In fact, he hit the road of high expectations with verve.

Aaron bristles at all the new age "drivel" about stress. Some softies in his office moan about the brutal pace. He thrives on it and believes that there is nothing better than that rush of adrenalin. It makes him feel alive. When his assistant asked for time off to go to a stress-reduction seminar, he scoffed, "That touchy-feely stuff won't get you anywhere. Take the Peak Performance program I did so well at. Great strategies on how to achieve more, in less time."

(Aaron neglects to disclose that he suffers from panic attacks. He wakes up in the middle of the night—he does sleep after all—in a sweat and with his heart pounding furiously. He has taken himself off to emergency for his "heart attack," only to be told that there is nothing wrong with his heart.)

There is no such thing as time off for Aaron. He is "on" all the time. Even though his mum and dad are gone, the child in him still longs for their approval. He doesn't realize this deep need fuels much of his ambition. The inner voice that says, "Keep going till you drop" is no longer even in his awareness. His focus is outside. His eye is on the ball. He is determined to win the game. Any game. Even when he plays games with his kids, he has to win.

Aaron is very attracted to Kim and projects his ideal onto her. She will not be as demanding as his ex-wife. She will be more like his mother. She is quiet. She will provide a calm oasis in his stressful life. She will be good with his kids.

STEP 2

Cut Back on Caffeine

What does caffeine do to harm you? Plenty. As little as two and a half cups per day can double the adrenalin in your bloodstream.

Peter G. Hanson, M.D.
The Joy of Stress

Our Favourite Fuel

I WAS MAKING $100,000 A YEAR, I HAD 75 PEOPLE UNDER ME, A CONDO IN ASPEN, AND WAS BEING CONSIDERED FOR THE SENATE, AND THEN I SWITCHED TO DECAF.

Frank & Ernest reprinted by permission of Newspaper Enterprise Association Inc.

He jangled the coins in his pocket, shifted in his chair and crossed his arms. "I'm not going to tell you," he asserted. I had just asked Frank, the high-powered coronary patient, about his caffeine use during a "routine intake" —the initial interview—at the cardiac clinic.

Years of professional training enabled me to pose the next question, "Why won't you tell me?"

"Because you wouldn't believe me," he allowed.

I paused—another advanced interviewing technique—and soon he confessed, "I drink about 30 cups of coffee a day."

Trying hard to maintain my professional calm, I stuttered, "Are you sure?"

"Yep. I get up at seven and drink about three cups an hour, for the next ten hours."

Although I have counselled thousands of patients, I had never heard anything like this. There had been, however, Amanda, who was very conscientious, a hard worker, and who often had debilitating migraines. She told me she didn't take any caffeine. "No coffee or tea. Never touch the stuff." But with a little more prodding, I discovered she drank 16 cups of diet cola a day!

Caffeine jump-starts our weary system in the morning. It's a reliable pick-me-up during the day. We offer a "cuppa" to our guests, arrange to meet our friends for cappuccino and treat ourselves to a cola on a hot day.

However, what caffeine addicts often don't know is this drug works on the nervous system in much the same way as the stress response, takes a toll on the system and, ironically, drains energy reserves. They don't need to depend on this artificial fuel. In Step 6 you'll see a selection of energy-boosting fuels that are natural, not habit forming and very good for your health.

I have seen dramatic changes in Type A's who have reduced their caffeine intake—not only in their ability to manage stress but in personality style. If it weren't for all those *lattes grande*, you might be a very mellow person.

As you may know, unhealthy A's often rely on caffeine to fuel the never-let-up pace. And we Type A's have, if I may say, a tendency to overdo things and to ignore messages from our body. When we're ready to collapse from overwork, we flog our system as if it were a dead horse. Using caffeine to override fatigue is very hard on the body. The energy sag, which we're trying to avoid, is healthy; our system pulls the plug to put us in a much-needed recharge mode. This "drive-until-you-drop" attitude can lead to burn-out.

Some people refuse to take this seriously. In one of my Relax/Recharge groups, a person offered, "Do you know why Irish coffee is the perfect food? It has the four main food groups: alcohol, caffeine, sugar and fat."

Let's not lose our sense of humour, but if you're experiencing some of the following symptoms, you might consider them a wake-up call.

- Increased stress levels (scored in the high range in the Signs of Stress questionnaire)
- Irritability, feeling jittery and on edge
- Shaky hands, trembling
- Difficulty falling asleep
- Headache if you go without caffeine
- Dependence on caffeine for energy in the morning or at other times

Now, there's no need to clutch your treasured coffee mug protectively. This is a safe drug *in moderation* for most people, but can be trouble when consumed in excess. I just want you to be informed, and perhaps to ask for natural decaf more often.

I interviewed some of my colleagues practising here in Victoria and asked for their insights and recommendations.

Caffeine and the Heart

Rick Leather, M.D., a cardiologist, cautions:

> Like any stimulant, caffeine acts like adrenalin on the heart. It can make your heart beat faster and harder—tachycardia, or palpitations. It can also affect rhythm, and if someone has an abnormal heart, caffeine may exacerbate arrhythmia. It can increase blood pressure—this effect is magnified if you also smoke. If someone has unstable heart problems, I prefer them to stay away from caffeine altogether. If they are stable, moderate use is fine—a cup or two a day. Most cardiac patients don't take caffeine.

The U.S. *Journal of Clinical Epidemiology* reported in 1992 that a series of studies found a significant association between coffee consumption and all cardiovascular diseases. In one study, people who drank more than five cups of coffee a day were twice as likely to have heart attacks as non-drinkers.

Caffeine and Migraine

Alex Moll, M.D., a neurologist, reports:

> Blood vessels initially constrict when caffeine is ingested. This may assist in migraine pain relief. When medications containing caffeine are taken repetitively, for instance one or more times daily—the blood vessel constriction may be followed by a rebound of excessive dilation of the vessel. This brings the headache back with renewed strength after a few hours of pain relief. Certain migraine preparations, such as Cafergot, AC & C, 222, 282, 292, 642, Tylenol #1, 2, & 3, contain caffeine to reduce the throbbing migraine pain. Repetitive use of these medications on a daily basis may thus set the migraine sufferer up for their next painful

headache. The condition known as Chronic Daily Headache, Medication Induced Headache or Analgesic Rebound Headache may be produced in this way.

Caffeine and Chi

Hong Zhu, M.D. (China), an acupuncturist, details the Traditional Chinese Medicine view:

> TCM holds that maintaining the balance of yin and yang energy is integral to the normal function of the human body. Too much yin or yang energy can cause illness. Coffee is a substance that is very yang, and, if taken in excess, upsets the normal balance of yin and yang, causing a condition known as "yang rising." This is manifested by such signs and symptoms as trembling hands, headaches, palpitations, anger, or impatience.
>
> In the context of Chinese herbalism, coffee is considered to be warm in nature (this has nothing to do with its temperature). Drinking too much coffee may cause "heat conditions." For the Chinese, tea is the beverage of choice. It is "cool" in nature and avoids the problems associated with coffee and cola drinks. Caffeine also causes a yo-yo effect on your blood sugar, which affects energy levels.

Caffeine and Nutrition

Joe Campbell, Ph.D., a nutritionist, has this to say about caffeine:

1. In excess, a condition known as caffeinism may result. Symptoms can be depression, high blood pressure, nervousness, heart palpitation, irritability, recurrent headaches and insomnia.
2. Irritates the entire urogenital tract.
3. Causes loss of the B and C vitamins and the mineral calcium.
4. When [caffeine is] combined with sugar, the loss of calcium is almost doubled and can contribute to osteoporosis, especially for post-menopausal women.
5. Interferes with the absorption of other essential minerals, especially magnesium and iron.
6. Can cause an elevation in cholesterol and triglycerides.

Caffeine and Women's Health

Frances Wren, M.D., an obstetrician/gynecologist, details:

> Caffeine, like cigarettes, can affect the absorption of calcium. And we want pregnant women to have more calcium and iron. Caffeine can also make people more agitated and not eat and sleep as well. It can also aggravate PMS; is linked with benign fibrocystic breast disease—people with this condition report the cysts dramatically reduce in size when they cut back on caffeine; may accelerate bone loss in post-menopausal women; may increase risk of miscarriage; crosses placenta and affects fetus for up to 3 days, appears in breast milk, hard for baby to metabolize (pregnancy and use of birth control pills double the length of time it takes the body to get rid of caffeine).

Caffeine and Stress

James Houston, M.D., a general practitioner with a special interest in complementary medicine, informs:

> This powerful drug has a diuretic effect and the body needs water for proper functioning, flushing wastes and toxins from the system, and maintaining a proper balance of fluid in the cells and bloodstream. Inadequate water intake may lead to kidney stones. Caffeine also aggravates stomach ulcers.
>
> It's important to look at why you are consuming the caffeine. It can be part of a whole picture—a way to cope with fatigue that we need to work with. Caffeine does not allow for the normal flow of energy through the body, and can easily add more stress to the whole system. I recommend no more than two cups a day.

The *American Journal of Psychiatry* published a study on the effects of caffeine on anxiety disorders including panic attacks and depression. In depressed people caffeine can induce anxiety. And stress levels can increase when patients with panic symptoms ingest caffeine.

Enough already? So maybe you don't have heart disease or panic attacks, but if you seriously want to become a healthier Type A, asking for decaf *lattes* is one of the best steps you can take. As you'll see from the chart on the following page, caffeine pops up in some surprising places.

Caffeine Chart

Multiply the amount, in milligrams (mg), of caffeine you have on an *average* day by the number of servings. Caffeine in tea and coffee varies with method of brewing, the kind and brand. Note the size of cup or mug.

Coffee	Number of cups	Reg. teacup 6 oz.	Med. mug 8 oz.	Large mug 12 oz.	Total
Drip		105	140	200	
Instant		60	80	120	
Decaf		6	8	12	
		Single	Double		
Espresso, Latte		100	200		
Cappuccino, etc.		100	200		
Cappuccino, decaf		5	10		
Tea					
Tea – brewed 3 minutes		40	53	80	
Instant tea		30	40	60	
Decaf tea		1	1.3	2	

Soft Drinks	Number of 12 oz. bottles or cans	mg of caffeine	Total
Coke		46	
Diet Coke		46	
Mountain Dew		55	
Pepsi		37	
Diet Pepsi		36	
Perrier, club soda, tonic water, 7-Up, ginger ale, juices, mineral water contain no caffeine			

Total _____

Sources: American Dietetic Association; Bowes and Church's Food Values, 17th ed. 1998.

Minimizing Withdrawal

As with other drugs—I know you never inhaled, neither did I—you build up a tolerance to caffeine. The reason you can merrily consume five or six servings a day and still feel in control is that you have "habituated" to that level.

If you were to stop your caffeine intake for several weeks and then one day drink your usual amount, you would feel jittery, anxious and speedy. These are the same symptoms you'd suffer if you were having a panic attack.

Don't despair. For most of us, caffeine in moderation is fine. And the good news is that if you cut back significantly, you'll adapt to lower levels and get the same buzz from much less.

The best time for a caffeine hit is in the morning. The worst time is in the evening. Offer natural decaf after supper and more guests will join you.

How much is too much? If you had a high score on the Signs of Stress questionnaire or have health problems, more than one cup a day may be too much. For most of us, two cups of coffee or four teas is a reasonable amount. Make sure you take soft drinks, chocolate and drugs that contain caffeine into account.

Suggestions for Cutting Back

Add up your daily total on the chart. Note the serving sizes: a regular teacup is 6 ounces, a regular mug is 8 ounces and a tall mug is 12 ounces. (A *grande* is 16 ounces.)

- Week 1—drink one-quarter less than your usual amount (if you usually drink eight cups a day, try six)
- Week 2—reduce by another quarter (to four cups)
- Week 3—reduce by a final quarter (to two cups)

Adjustment to this final level may take several weeks.

Cut Back Gradually

If you go cold turkey, you may get a pounding headache. Caffeine narrows blood vessels, and during withdrawal these vessels can overdilate and give you a migraine. (This is why some people get a headache on the weekend; they are not drinking as much caffeine at home as they do at work.)

You may feel more tired at first, while your system adapts. Hang in there. Soon you'll be less tense and you'll sleep better—this will recharge your batteries and rouse more of your natural fuel. Soon you will feel calm and have lots of energy.

With much less caffeine, Frank is transformed; still high in energy, he is not as easily angered and takes things as they come. Amanda is still conscientious but has eased up on pressuring herself, has given up cola and rarely has a migraine.

When you're feeling really low and sluggish, get out and breathe some fresh air. Breathe deeply. Swing your arms. Activity gets your cardiovascular system going, your blood flowing. With more oxygen, you have more energy. You have so much more life force to tap into—you don't need to depend on caffeine and sugar for fuel.

Decaf—Better or Worse?

The last straw was a report that decaffeinated coffee was toxic and might be implicated in cancer! Let me clear that one up first. Methylene chloride, a solvent reported to cause cancer in laboratory animals, was the agent used most often.

You'll be relieved to see *naturally decaffeinated* on many labels. Ask for it. Water or steam is used in this process and takes out the caffeine while leaving in the taste. If you have stomach problems, however, you might have to switch to other beverages because the acid content remains high.

The best-quality decaf products come from health food or specialty stores; there is a wide range of naturally decaffeinated beverages: black teas, herbal teas, no-caffeine beverages and steam-processed coffee—the really pure stuff is decaffeinated in the clear air of the high Alps by virgins, in the early dawn. This is why it's so expensive these days.

STEP 3

Take Stock of Your Stress

All illnesses should be assumed to be stress-related until proven otherwise. Even if stress is not the primary cause of illness, it is frequently an aggravating factor. To say that a bodily complaint is stress-related does not in any way mean that it is unreal or unimportant; it simply means that time spent at stress reduction and relaxation training may be very worthwhile in terms of obtaining relief.

Andrew Weil, M.D.
Spontaneous Healing

A Fast-Paced Life Can Slow You Down

The never-let-up pressure is taking its toll: furrowed brow, greying hair, thickening waist. Days are brutal, nights are late. And after years of hard work, Kirk is still struggling to keep his business afloat. His stomach burns, his back aches, his stamina is fading, his patience is wearing thin and he can't sleep at night—unmistakable signs of strain, but he ignores them. Or he tries to.

You've seen this Type A go-getter, or someone just like him, around town, with a cell phone in one hand and a coffee mug in the other. Whenever clients call, he's there. Day. Night. Weekends. He knows he's getting short tempered with his staff, but feels unjustly maligned when they grumble about his forceful style. After all, he gets things done. If he weren't so hard driving, his employees would be out of a job, right?

There's more pressure waiting for him at home. His wife, Beverly, begs him to unplug. "That's easier said than done," he grumbles. And he resents the nagging. His kids plead with him to take a day off. Don't they appreciate that he's doing this for them?

And he doesn't want to hear any more about being a workaholic. It's not that he's so competitive or so driven. He has to keep up this pace simply to keep all the plates spinning.

Jolts of caffeine kick-start his flagging system each morning. Belts of scotch uncoil his inner knots each evening. He falls into bed in an exhausted heap, but wakes up after a few hours. Shifting from position to position, he fails to find one that will push him over the edge into much-needed slumber. He watches the clock tick mercilessly until dawn. "It's time to get some strong sleeping pills," he resolves.

For years, Beverly has tried to get Kirk to see a doctor. So she's surprised the next morning when he asks her to make an appointment for him.

"Your blood pressure is too high," the doctor warns, "You need to lose weight. You must eat better and get more exercise. And it's time to take control of the stress in your life. These things will help lower your blood pressure and help you sleep, too. Better than relying on pills."

"Not for me," Kirk grumbles. "Diet . . . exercise . . . who's got the time? All I really need is a good night's sleep once in awhile. Can't you give me something for that?"

"Being busy is one thing," replies his doctor. "Burning yourself out is another. I can give you a prescription, but unless you address the cause of these symptoms, you may find things get worse."

"Worse? What could be worse than being in pain during the day and lying awake at night?"

"Lots of things," the doctor continues, "You know there's a history of heart disease in your family. Your high blood pressure and your tendency to hostility put you at risk of a heart attack. Think about it."

"What hostility?" Kirk shoots back and stomps out of the office. His pager goes off. He takes the call on his car phone, but his mind is far away. Bits of the conversation with the doctor come back to him throughout the day.

He remembers the shock a few years ago when a fellow at work—his age—just dropped dead. And his father wasn't much older than he is now when he had his fatal heart attack. His mother died of breast cancer a few years earlier. By the time he gets home, he's done a lot of thinking.

"Well, you're right," he commends Beverly as he strides past her, picking up the mail in one hand and the newspaper in the other. "The doctor says I'm working too hard, too." He decides to leave out the stuff about the heart attack risk.

"Please listen to him," Beverly begs. She wonders, as she says this, if she's getting through. Can Kirk be listening to her while he's sorting through the mail and turning on the television?

Kirk's sister Marie shares many of his traits and many of his challenges. Marie—remember her from the introduction?—has always been a take-charge leader. Even in school she was the first on the baseball field and the first to organize the group. "Now, you play first base. You be the back catcher..." With her quick mind and powerful energy she was formidable on the junior high debating team. She gave this up in high school, however, as she was increasingly interested in the best-looking guys. It was irritating, even then, when someone told her she was "coming on too strong."

Today, Marie runs her own business and is proud of its success. She is fond of the people who work for her and would be very hurt if she heard how they complain about her high-pressure style.

"Do you think she ever slows down?" asks Susan, one of the front office staff.

Marie's assistant, Emily, replies, "Yeah, I've seen her crash. If you call that slowing down."

"I don't know how you take it. Getting barked at. She sounds like a drill sergeant."

Emily asserts, "I don't mind so much. I know she's a softie underneath."

"Must be pretty far underneath. She always looks so tense, so in control. So perfect. I can't imagine she ever goes through the emotional stuff we do."

This is just one of the myths about Marie. Because she is so decisive, people don't see her vulnerability, don't realize she's barely holding everything together.

She gets debilitating headaches, but manages to keep this hidden from most of her staff. And she is turning more and more to alcohol to relax— a common and dangerous trap. Despite the history of heart disease and cancer in her family she doesn't allow these or other troubling thoughts into her mind.

Marie, who has lost touch with her old friends, no longer takes the time to do the fun things she used to do to unwind. And the more time she devotes to her work, the more out of touch she gets. The lopsidedness and stress in her life are not only making her more unhappy, they are draining her energy and endangering her health. Marie doesn't realize that her immune system is suppressed—that's why it takes her so long to recover from a cold or flu.

Is Life Trying to Stress You Out Too?

Even as a so-called stress expert, I work with life's aggravations with varying degrees of success.

Here's a typical scenario: I'm on the phone in search of some documents and a merchant number so we can accept bank card payments for a series of upcoming public seminars. "Yes, we can do that for you," the confident-sounding voice assures me. "No need to make an appointment."

The midday downtown traffic is congested. Finally, I find a parking space. Since this is going to take only a few minutes, should I put a whole loonie in the meter? I don't have one, so I settle for two quarters.

The bank is packed. The pleasant-looking person at the counter points at the appropriate queue. Obediently, I take my place. And wait. This line is not exactly zooming forward. After 20 minutes—one quarter in the meter gone—I reach my destination, in reasonably fine fettle. I tell the young woman what I need.

"Oh," she blinks at me, "I don't know how to do that! You have to see Ms. Blank. Do you have an appointment?"

I try to exhale some of the steam building up inside and explain that I was told I didn't need an appointment.

"I don't know who would have told you that," she replies, as if I'm making it up. "Ms. Blank has someone with her. If you would like to wait in that line over there, you might catch her between appointments."

An inner debate rattles on: "Is it better to forget this now and come back later? Or is that going to be more aggravation?" I decide to stick it out. Another 20 minutes drag by. (Why does time snatched out of your day for a tea break go so quickly, and the same amount of time spent standing in a line go so slowly?)

Finally, the person who had been going on and on and on, blissfully ignorant of my fixed stare boring into her back, closes her briefcase. That's a hopeful sign. No. She has a few more questions.

I do more of my famous relaxation breathing. This helps. I am now more settled. She leaves. I seize the moment and dart into Ms. Blank's office.

"I need to get a merchant's number," I blurt out, before she has a chance to speak. I fire off all the details of what I need.

"Sorry," she says, not looking sorry at all. "If you don't have a retail store, we can't help you here."

By this time I've become convinced that neither she nor her co-workers are real people, who have lives, who go home at night to their families.

No, these are surreal beings who appear human during the day, but who, after hours, retreat into a large underground, windowless room to plot increasingly creative ways to frustrate us. And they have succeeded today.

They've infiltrated the phone company too! Back at my office, I call the bank's Vancouver office. I'm told they don't have an 800 number. I can call collect. The phone company's automated operator at this end rings the number and when the call is answered goes through its paces: "You have a collect call from—'Kerry Crofton.' To accept this collect call, please press one."

My call has been answered by an automated voice machine on the other end: "For service in English, please press one; to get information about your account please press two."

I listen helplessly as these two machines talk at each other. There is no room for me to participate. (Fortunately, my own bank intervenes. They must have secret numbers they can use to get through to real people.)

Are these automated devices expressly designed to frustrate us? And what about all that hoopla about the great burden of leisure time, increased efficiency and decreased amount of paper that this technological age was supposed to bring?

Few of the organizations we have to deal with seem to care very much about what we really care about—getting through *our* day. It can be frustrating. I'm going out to weed the garden. Or to yank out anything that looks like a weed!

Stress and the Healthy Type A

Dr. Hans Selye, a Canadian medical researcher, first defined stress as "a non-specific response of the body to meet a demand made upon it." Selye also described stress as "the spice of life." This gearing up of the body, he explained, was not always harmful, but sometimes necessary and healthy.

Channelling this primal energy in a positive direction is the foundation for becoming a healthy Type A. This poses a particular challenge since we Type A's have a naturally reactive system and are prone to overheating with the intensity of our red-hot energy.

Type A's are sometimes called "hot reactors" because of this tendency to react to people and things that get in the way with bursts of hostility or anger. The hot reactor style is hazardous to their health: there's strong evidence to suggest that hot reactors respond to stress with a sudden spike in blood pressure, even if they seem calm on the outside. And a new report on a 20-year study of 750 men done at Duke University, in North Carolina, indicates that men who are "socially dominant"—who interrupt, are pushy and always compete for attention—are far more likely to die from heart attacks, strokes and high blood pressure than their calmer colleagues.

Even when many overextended A's are so tired they have trouble getting out of bed in the morning, even when they're plagued with a plethora of stress-related conditions and even when they rely more and more on booze, antidepressants, tranquillizers and sleeping pills, they still don't realize they have too much stress.

A Fast-Paced Life Is Hard on Relationships

In some cases, stress can kill—through heart disease and strokes. More often, it can weaken the immune system, making us more susceptible to colds and flu, chronic fatigue and even cancer. Stress affects every system and every cell of the body.

Stress contributes to headaches, numerous gastrointestinal disorders, high blood pressure and other cardiovascular conditions such as angina. It drains our energy, ages us and wreaks havoc with our emotions.

It's Friday evening and Kirk and Beverly are both beat. It's an unpleasant mix of being keyed up and wrung out. They're determined to do something together because they want to feel that they have a life.

"Let's watch TV," Beverly suggests.

"Nah. There's nothing good on," Kirk complains.

"Let's get a video."

"Okay. But I want to walk to the video store."

"Nah. It's too far. You don't seem to realize how tired I am. How hard I work."

"You think you're the only one who works hard. You don't appreciate how hard I work."

And on it goes...

You are both at the end of your energy tether. You are overly sensitive and it's too easy for little grievances to solidify into major conflicts. Things escalate when you're stressed. You lose your patience, cheerfulness, humour and softness. Part of you may even welcome a confrontation so you can blow off some of that pent-up steam.

There are times when you should just say, "I'm wiped out. I'd really like to soak in a hot tub for a while and go to bed early with a good book. I do love you. Let's do something fun together tomorrow, when we have more energy."

The cost of too much stress to ourselves, to our relationships and to our society is tremendous.

As I mentioned earlier, physicians estimate that between 70 and 80 percent of all the conditions that they see are stress related. This is a tremendous burden on health care budgets, as well as an enormous cost to business and industry in absenteeism and decreased productivity.

As you glance down the list on the following page, see whether these conditions affect you.

The Pressure Cooker below Decks

Years ago, in Halifax, I did a study on stress and the Canadian navy maritime engineers. These fellows were called "stokers," a term derived from the days when their early counterparts would stoke the engines with coal.

Those stokers below decks (like your nervous system) rely on the captain on the bridge (your brain) to give orders. The stokers, or your nervous system, can't see what's going on and can't tell if there is a real or imagined threat when ordered to rev up the engines. This is a crucial distinction.

If it is a real threat—an enemy is approaching—you launch a frontal attack or slip away to a safe harbour. In either case, you use up all that fuel (adrenalin). Afterwards, you return to normal and gear down.

If, however, the threat is an irritating boss, you gear up but hold back from acting upon your impulses. Without vigorous muscular activity to release the adrenalin, you continue to steam inside. Pressure builds up— with no release—to the detriment of your health. This situation is not a problem when we get a bit upset occasionally, if we can let it go; it is a problem when we get very upset often and we stay upset and cling to our resentments.

When you gear up appropriately, meet the challenge and then gear down, you're using the stress energy effectively. This is how this survival mechanism was intended to work. It was not intended to do us in.

Stress-Related Conditions

Check the ones which are, or have been, a significant problem.

Note: Not everything on the list is 100 percent stress related. But mismanaged stress is a factor.

___ Tension headaches
___ Muscle spasm
___ Back pain
___ Teeth grinding – bruxism
___ Nervous tics
___ Acid stomach
___ Heartburn
___ Irritable bowel syndrome
___ Ulcerative colitis
___ Crohn's disease
___ Diarrhea, constipation
___ Post-traumatic stress disorder
___ Nervousness
___ Hyperventilation
___ Insomnia
___ Depression
___ Suicide
___ Panic attacks
___ Migraine
___ Reynaud's disease
___ High blood pressure
___ Dizziness
___ Angina pectoris – chest pain
___ "False alarm" heart attacks
___ Coronary artery disease
___ Heart attack/stroke
___ Arrhythmia – irregular heartbeat
___ Tachycardia – palpitations

___ Susceptibility to infections
___ Recurrent low-grade infections
___ Frequent colds and flu
___ Hives
___ Herpes
___ Strep throat
___ Sores in mouth
___ Mononucleosis
___ Fatigue, low energy
___ Yeast symptoms
___ Allergies
___ Cancer
___ Arthritic joint pain
___ Diabetes
___ Decreased sex drive
___ Sexual dysfunction

"Mr. White is here for his annual checkup, doctor."

How It Used to Be

So there you are, a cave-dweller 50,000 years ago sitting around the camp-fire in the evening, gnawing on bones, picking lice off your mate (no TV to watch, no newspapers to read—what else is there to do?). You freeze. On the spot. There's a sabre-toothed tiger.

Now, you're not going to pause and reflect, "Tiger . . . let me think . . . is that one of those *dangerous* animals?"

In an instant, our self-preservation kicks in and triggers a barrage of physiological responses from the sympathetic nervous system, what I call the "go mode."

Meanwhile, the tiger is going through a similar process: "Ah! Dinner." Its heart is pumping faster, spurred on by the adrenalin; it braces its muscles, getting ready to pounce. It's baring its fangs; its fur is standing on end to make it look more menacing.

You're frightened and generating a lot of heat. Your thermostat signals the cooling mechanism. You sweat.

Now is the time for battle. Therefore, the non-essential functions of the parasympathetic nervous system—what I call the "rest mode"—are put on hold.

Your digestion slows down. You have only so much blood and energy, and it's sent to the high-priority places, like the heart, lungs and big muscles, and taken away from the peripheral blood vessels and the gastrointestinal system. That bison meat sits pretty heavily in your stomach.

Stomach acid is also reduced but may come back stronger later and lead to hyperacidity. With chronic stress, these effects can lead to a variety of gastrointestinal disorders.

Focused on saving your life and that of your family, your stress hormones increase, at the expense of your sex hormones. You're supposed to be focused on saving your family's lives, not distracted by thoughts like, "Hey, you're looking good tonight."

With chronic stress, this "endocrine priority" can lead to many hormone-related problems such as a less-than-passionate sex life.

The immune system—our internal army of billions of cells working to ward off invaders and scavenge potential harmful garbage—is also suppressed. This suppression compromises the ability of the immune cells to fight off infection and to keep us healthy. This is very closely connected with our energy levels.

Highlights of the Go Mode

The go mode leaps into action when we feel challenged by a real or imagined threat. (It should be kept in reserve for those snarling tigers, not for snarled traffic.)

- "There's trouble out there." This thought is generated in the cortex of the brain.
- "Got to attack the enemy or run for cover." This instinct comes from the limbic system of the brain.
- The hypothalamus, a small part of your brain, hears the battle cry and spurs the pituitary gland into action; the pituitary then sounds the bugle to rouse the forces.
- The front half of the pituitary produces the stress hormone ACTH (adrenocorticotropic hormone). Now the troops are really fired up.

- ACTH goes into the bloodstream and, when it reaches the adrenal cortex, stimulates production of adrenalin.
- Adrenalin alerts the rest of the defences, and all systems are go.
- When the body has been supplied with enough of these defence hormones and you have either won the fight or escaped the danger, the hypothalamus senses this and shuts off the electrical signal to the back half of the pituitary. Your system is then ready for the next life-threatening encounter.

Resulting Conditions
- Heart beats strongly and rapidly to rev up the system. This can be a factor in tachycardia, arrhythmia, angina.
- Peripheral blood vessels constrict to divert blood to high-priority areas. This cools the hands and feet and is a factor in high blood pressure, Reynaud's disease and migraine headaches. (Yes, those cool hands and feet can be a result of chronic stress or a low thyroid. Not that easy to dismiss as "just poor circulation.")
- Blood thickens to keep you from bleeding to death if the tiger got a good chunk of you. This thicker, stickier blood can increase blood pressure and the risk of heart attack or stroke.
- Breathing quickens to get more oxygen and bronchial tubes constrict; this can bring on asthma attacks.
- Muscles tense. If there is no action and no release, the continual tightening can lead to chronic pain, spasm, injury, muscle dysfunction and muscle contraction headaches.
- Cortisol, another hormone, also gets the blood pressure going and increases cholesterol levels for energy. This hormone is the link between stress and high cholesterol.

Is There Such a Thing as Healthy Stress?

The stress response is connected to the primitive lower brain. Over the past fifty thousand years, our brains have changed considerably, and, as a species, we have developed higher centres of the brain. They're the so-called civilized, rational part of the brain that says, "No, don't club that person over the head . . . that's your boss . . . you need this job." (Now, as you know, if you've seen any fights in pubs, not everyone has completed this process.)

However, our nervous systems are still back in the neolithic period, even though they have to contend with modern-day stressors.

Let's say you and a friend are running to catch a bus. You're using up the adrenalin your body is producing for this vigorous muscular activity. When you get on the bus, you sit and gear down. "Thank Heavens we made it," you sigh.

You're beginning to cool off and catch your breath, your blood pressure and heart rate are coming down and levels of adrenalin are back to normal. No problem.

However, your friend is ticked off. "If that waiter hadn't taken so long with our meal, we wouldn't have had to rush to catch this bus. This kind of stuff just drives me crazy; there's no such thing as good service these days . . . and you're still expected to leave a tip. It makes me so mad. And the other thing that burns me up is . . ."

She's fuming about something that's past and that did not pose a threat. There's no action required so her nervous system is getting all steamed up. It thinks she's getting ready for battle. It hovers in the panic mode, on red alert.

That's the unhealthy stress. And, as you know, it zaps energy. Unfortunately, I see many cases of this battle fatigue today. And, in my findings, the threats are heavy workload, mismanaged change and uncertainty.

The heavy workload grinds you down because you have to sustain a high pitch of activity throughout the day and throughout the week. You're burning fuel at a rapid rate.

Change, mismanaged or not, can be extremely stressful. As Dr. Selye pointed out, humans and rats like consistency; they like the tasks they've mastered to stay pretty much the same. They also like to have the tools, skills and time required to complete the tasks. (Tell this to your boss.) Whether change occurs in job responsibilities or in family status and whether it's positive (like a much-desired new baby) or negative (such as a death in the family), change requires adaptation, which is stressful. This is especially true when it's a change over which we have no control.

Uncertainty is equally stressful. You thrive on security, and it's very troubling to your system when this is threatened: will you be laid off in the next round of cuts? Will you be able to sell the house? Should you cash in your RRSP and try to set out on your own? What will happen to you? To your family? To your mortgage payments?

When you're facing an immediate threat, like chasing after someone who stole your bicycle, you react by gearing up to take action. Then it's over, and you gear down. No problem. It's the ongoing, uncertain, out-of-your-control, but very real, threats to your security that significantly undermine physical and emotional well-being.

The resulting emotions brought on by this threat—fear, frustration, impatience and anger—are draining. In the later stages of the exhaustion phase even these strong emotions flatten out. Apathy takes hold. You feel empty. At the time when you most need to take care of yourself, you couldn't care less.

Over the long term, this constant pattern of being all fired up with nowhere to run has potentially serious consequences.

System Burn-out—Why We Feel So Exhausted

Burn-out affects men and women at every level of employment. Those professionals that suffer the most burn-out include physicians, judges, public administrators, accountants, credit managers, bond dealers, air traffic controllers and corporate managers. Burn-out is even more common in people within the helping professions such as nursing, teaching and social work.

Christina Maslach, a researcher at the University of California, says burn-out has three phases.

1. Emotional exhaustion: a feeling of being drained or used up, and of having nothing more to give
2. Cynicism: a callous, insensitive regard for people
3. Hopelessness: the belief that the individual has been unsuccessful and that all effort has been fruitless

Burn-out happens when the adrenal glands and just about every cell in the body are "exhausted." Running out of steam happens to all of us once in awhile. You don't want to talk to anyone. You don't want to do anything. Then, after a few days of rest and relaxation, you recover and are ready to hit the road again. But what happens when you run on empty for too long? when a brief break is not enough to recharge?

Dr. Herbert Freudenberger, the author of several books on burn-out, describes this state as, "the body says no but the head says go." This is not a lapse of motivation from a weak-willed mind: it is the result of chronic overstimulation of the sympathetic nervous system—too many spurts of the gearing-up hormones, including adrenalin.

Dr. Hong Zhu, an acupuncturist in Victoria, offers the TCM perspective:

> We treat stress symptoms and long-term stress differently. When it reaches the burn-out stage, it is considered quite a deep condition that requires working on the root. The root is the kidney. Burn-out, in TCM terms, is called Kidney Yang Energy Deficiency. A dysfunction in the pituitary/adrenal system is part of this deficiency. The symptoms include no energy, poor circulation, foggy thinking. The thyroid hormones could also be affected. Treatment is with acupuncture and herbs to warm the kidneys and increase circulation.

Dr. James Houston, a Victoria physician, warns,

> Dealing with pressure and anxiety over time can lead to chronic stress. The resulting overproduction of adrenal hormones does much damage, including increasing free radicals which harm all the tissues

in the body. If this situation continues over long periods of time, there's a decrease in the production of the adrenal hormones—adrenal exhaustion.

This produces fatigue and other symptoms and compromises the body's ability to keep responding. Then, there is further long-term damage to the organs, connective tissue and immune system. The kidneys, for example, are affected by the increased production of residue toxins or waste products which they must filter.

The following statements are signs of various stages of burn-out. Do any of these apply to you?

- I feel crowded in.
- My sense of humour is gone.
- My fuse is shorter.
- I get frustrated more often.
- I feel tired, overworked, overwhelmed.
- I'm often depressed.
- I am smoking or drinking more.
- I'm eating more sugar to get more energy.
- I'm drinking more coffee to keep myself going.
- I don't seem to care as much about others, about myself, about anything.
- I avoid intimacy and have lost interest in sex.
- I have lost my perspective; little things become insurmountable obstacles.
- I want to crawl into bed, pull up the covers and make the world go away.
- I'm on medications for depression or anxiety, or to help me sleep.
- I feel empty.
- Life seems overwhelming and pointless. I sometimes have thoughts of "ending it all."

There is no rating score here because even one of these might be a sign that you need to recharge.

If you take the time to reflect, you will know instinctively that it's time to do something. Or, rather, it's time to gear down and do nothing. (Another lost art.) The good news is burn-out is not "in your head," and it can be treated. As with many things, prevention is the best cure. If you know someone who is on the downhill slope to burn-out, please help them take charge and recharge.

Reduce Your Stress

One of the body's most remarkable means of regulating its own physiological machinery is a stress-reducing phenomenon we call the relaxation response... Many studies have now shown that in people who regularly elicit the relaxation response, there is a decrease in anxiety, anger, and hostility, as well as depression.

Herbert Benson, M.D.
in *Mind/Body Medicine*, edited by Daniel Goleman, Ph.D., and Joel Gurin

Do you tune in to your stress in time to do something before it overtakes you? I hope so because this is one of the most worthwhile challenges we A's will ever face. And given that most Type A's have an innate talent for mastering new things, you shouldn't have too much difficulty with gearing down.

The following 25 techniques and strategies are ones that I have used for two decades with many Type A's—including myself. These strategies have three objectives: to reduce the baseline of your stress level, so you live with less tension, day to day; to reduce the intensity of your response—not to make you dull and detached, but so you don't hit the roof over little things (even big ones); and to reduce the time it takes you to recover, to cool down.

1. Know Your Dashboard

I often say we should have been born with a dashboard. Well, in a sense, we were—it's just that most of us have never learned much about it. Your dashboard looks something like this.

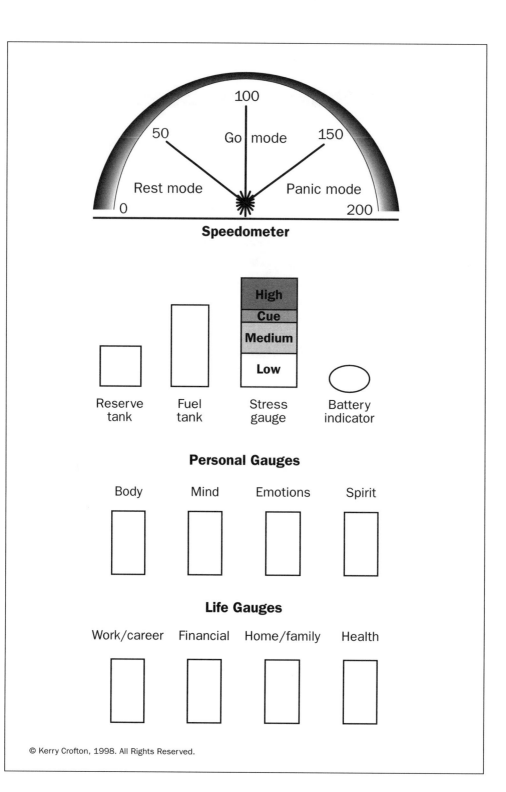

All right, so you're not a car. But it's true that the performance you can expect out of your car—or yourself—has a lot to do with how you treat it, what you use for fuel and how often you pause to refuel.

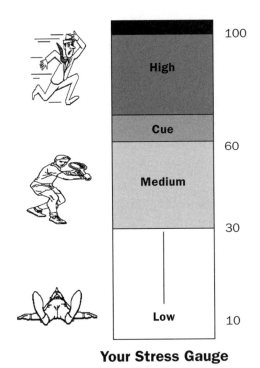

Your Stress Gauge

Your stress gauge is front and centre on your dashboard. The low zone is relaxation, or the rest mode, when you feel at ease, calm and settled. It's good to experience this mode often—and drug-free.

In the middle is the "joy of stress" zone, as described by Dr. Peter Hanson. You are charged up, inspired and inspiring—just the right amount of gearing up. You've got all those plates spinning in the air. No problem. You feel alive. You feel on top of things. You're well seated, riding your spirited Type A energy.

As you heat up and rise into the high zone, you're beginning to get too revved up. Your engine begins to overheat. You forget things. You bark at people. You feel . . . well, you know how you feel. Like screaming? There is however, a golden opportunity before you hit this zone. An opportunity to seize.

2. Know Your Stress Cue

Our smart old nervous system has a built-in early-warning mechanism that sets off an increasingly loud series of alarms. We call them symptoms and usually try to ignore them or to silence them with medication.

At first, sotto voce, the warning signal begins to call to us. This subtle alarm is usually drowned out by the cacophony of daily life. In your body, this stage would be represented by a slight tensing of the muscles.

As your tension crescendoes, there is a tightening of the jaw, a clenching of the fist or a pain in the back of your neck. You might reach for painkillers to put a stop to all that. Or you might ignore the warning.

Listen to the inner voice pleading with you, "Your stress gauge is getting too high. Please step back and breathe and gear down. In the big picture, this doesn't matter. Let it go.

My warning signal is a racing feeling, as if hamsters were tearing around in my stomach. In the past, I ignored the cue and took action only when I had stomach pains. Now, I'm on to them and just before those hamsters take off above the speed limit, I pause and breathe. It does work.

When I'm giving a presentation, I need to be geared up; it takes a lot of energy to keep the audience's attention. But if I'm geared up too much, I talk too quickly and race through my material, leaving my audience and myself breathless. Regulating my stress gauge is something I work with all the time.

These four steps are the heart of reducing stress:
1. know your stress cue
2. listen to your stress cue
3. breathe and gear down
4. let it go

Please jot these steps down on a piece of paper and post it where you'll see it often: on your computer, on your phone, in your car—on your fridge?

3. Tune in to Your Stress Cue

There are three important points to remember. First, your cue needs to be early. Remember the fellow with the chest pains? By the time you're getting symptoms like that, you have missed a long series of cues. By the time you have a headache or a bout of insomnia, your cues, such as tensing muscles, have gone unheeded for some time. The secret is to tune in earlier and earlier until you are sensitive enough to wake up to a nuance of tension. The earlier you act, the easier it is to melt the tension away.

Second, your cue needs to be specific. "Feeling tense" or "getting angry" is too general.

Third, your cue needs to be physical. You bite the inside of your lip, your stomach gets knotted up, you hold your breath. Physical cues are easier to recognize.

The Challenge: You're feeling overwhelmed and worrying how you're going to get everything done. You're focused on the problem. Then you notice your cue, your neck is very tight. Then you have a choice.
The Choice:
• Keep on pushing, or
• Take charge. Breathe, gear down and then do some gentle stretching. See the futility of your worrying. Say to yourself, Let it go.

The Challenge: You're fuming angry at someone who was supposed to do something and hasn't.
The Choice:
• Keep complaining, or
• Take charge. Breathe out some of that steam. Walk some of it off if you can. Breathe deeply. Gear down. Say to yourself, Let it go.

Let what go? No, not your job. Not your responsibilities. Let go of a little of your obsession with things going your way. "This is how we do it," you insist. Why? Well. Because this is how you always do it. (This is what I call "narrow brain thinking.")

What if you let go of your preconceived, set-in-stone ideas? You might discover all sorts of new and creative things, and you leave room for others to be involved. They might get inspired and take some of the workload off you. This is a positive cycle and an excellent way to reduce your stress.

And what if you were to let go of some of the ground you have staked out in your relationships? What if you were to give the other person a little more room to be who they are instead of who you want them to be? Imagine how much that would reduce your stress and theirs.

Discover for yourself the magical effect of letting go the next time you are in a stress crunch. This is taking charge of your nervous system.

4. Come Down a Few Pegs to Lower Your Baseline

You're gripping the steering wheel, hurrying to a meeting or clutching the phone. Stop—you can do whatever you're doing at a more moderate level. How? Picture your stress gauge. If it's high, come down a few pegs; bring your stress gauge down from 70 to 50. Doing this often will make a world of difference in your life. This "economy of effort" is also an excellent fuel-conserving strategy. Your cue is an essential ally in developing awareness. (More on awareness in Step 9.)

5. Develop Your Stress Action Plan

Here's a short exercise. Finish these sentences:
- "I often overreact when..."
- "I know this is getting to me because I recognize my cue, which is..."
  (See the Signs of Stress quiz on page 2 for some suggestions.)
- "When I recognize my cue, I will..."

Recognizing your cue is the awareness. The next vital step is the action. Write down five on-the-spot tips you're ready to use. (Two weeks in the tropics would be very nice, but that's not much help right now.)

- _____
- _____
- _____
- _____
- _____

Here are some tips from creative go-getters who attended recent Healthy Type A workshops. Note the ones that you are ready to try.
- make time to slow down and breathe
- have more confidence in others and delegate
- learn to be patient
- don't try to do everything
- find ways to blow off steam
- be kinder to yourself
- learn that you can't change everything
- think before you speak
- learn to say no and walk away

- have more faith in yourself, no need to prove yourself all the time
- learn to channel anger
- learn to laugh and enjoy life
- count to ten, don't shoot from the lip
- take pride in being a Type A
- focus on the journey, not just the destination
- identify what can and cannot be changed
- don't try to please everyone
- slow down, step back, don't always try to take control
- don't be pushy, be more flexible
- lower your voice, be more soft spoken
- be more sensitive to others' feelings
- find a constructive outlet for excess energy
- expect obstacles and change
- don't take on unnecessary plates
- know your early warning sign and act on it
- choose a buddy to share a laugh with at work
- be less defensive of criticism
- do not overreact
- do not take on guilt and do not give it out
- be more considerate of Type B people
- be a team player, share knowledge and cooperate
- realize that you are expendable and replaceable
- don't try to change others into Type A's
- treat others as you would like them to treat you
- modify your style to suit the situation
- balance work and play
- schedule fewer activities
- be less impulsive
- make more time for the family
- have more compassion

All of the above are great wisdom from people like you. But you knew these things. The challenge is to use them. How? Create a conducive environment to break free of habitual patterns. Slowing down and being more awake—more conscious in the moment—will help put your resolve into action. Read on.

Some years ago, I worked with a high-powered group of ace fighter pilots at a U.S. Air Force base. My mission: to teach them to relax. These supremely confident flyers, with their steely-eyed concentration, are renowned for their fearlessness. In fact, they delight in ripping through the sky at supersonic speeds. Perhaps, at some time they even boasted that nothing would ever faze them. However, that was before they came to this stress management session.

During my session, each one listened intently, his sharp gaze focused on what I was saying. No problem. There followed a brief relaxation training exercise.

One fellow, his cool confidence shaken at the prospect of letting down his guard, sat bolt upright in his chair. Straight-armed, straight-legged, he braced himself in fierce anticipation of the potential danger of losing control. Instead of easing into the soothing calm of the rest mode, he was on red alert. When the five minutes were over, he eased up his taut grip on the chair and sighed heavily, "Whew. That was scary!"

After the initial fear of losing control, the fighter pilot did well in the training program. He was able to ease himself gently, toe by toe, into the unknown waters of relaxation. To his surprise, there was nothing lurking there to fear. In fact, he soon began to enjoy this letting go. "Reminds me of flying in my dad's glider, when I was young. The quiet, open space. Nothing going on. Just the vast blue stillness of the sky as far as you can see."

When Kirk started in this program he became very agitated during the relaxation training. High levels of adrenalin were still urging him into action. The more he was encouraged to let go, the more restless he became. Biofeedback was very helpful. (Biofeedback uses instruments that feed back detailed information on our reactions to stress to help us control these reactions.)

Aaron had the same challenge. Letting go of control, even when he claimed he wanted to, was very difficult. Kim had an easier time. She had a great appreciation of space and stillness, and found letting go with the breathing exercise very refreshing. She also moved quite quickly from Relaxation Training to the Mindfulness Meditation.

Frank really took to this gearing down, once he overcame the initial agitation. He set up a hammock in the backyard and now lies there for 15 minutes, morning and afternoon, doing his breathing relaxation. His blood pressure came down so much his doctor took him off the pills. "I've gone from medication to meditation," Frank boasts to his buddies.

The Foundation of Relaxation—Breathing

As babies, we were naturally deep breathers. But as we grew older and learned to repress our emotions, we were told, "Hold in that tummy!" (Remember when you could still do that?) As a result, our breathing became constricted and more shallow, and moved higher up in the chest. Rigid, controlled people tend to have rigid and controlled breathing. Even a slight shift in the way we breathe can become a most effective stress-reducing technique.

In 1975, a physician at Harvard Medical School, Dr. Herbert Benson, published an excellent book called *The Relaxation Response* (William Morrow and Company). What he describes as the relaxation response I call the rest mode.

Simply put, we have a rest mode as well as a go mode, and we have the option of shifting from one to the other. The best way to do that is with the relaxation technique called "belly breathing."

We try, in our own way, to get into the rest mode: we reach for a cigarette, a scotch, a cup of tea or coffee. None of these substances elicit the rest mode. Worse, these are "boomerangs"; they have the opposite effect.

It is vital for healthy A's to rely on natural, non-toxic ways to gear down into the rest mode. Relaxation breathing accesses the parasympathetic system—the quieting side of your nervous system. This is an untapped resource you can tune into at any time and, by doing so, enjoy these benefits:

- Calm nerves
- Lower blood pressure
- Slower heart rate and respiration
- Relaxed muscles and tension release
- A strengthened immune system
- A healthy gastrointestinal system
- Normal production of sex hormones
- A calmer mind and enhanced ability to let go of worries
- Stabilized emotions and a revived sense of humour
- Reduction in stress-related signs and conditions
- Recharged batteries and an uplifting sense of vitality
- Sound sleep

Relaxation breathing takes some practise and some patience, but is worth the effort. All of these benefits are accomplished without the side effects many people suffer when they take medications designed to produce the same results.

6. Learn the Amazing Feat of Belly Breathing

1. Sit in a comfortable chair that supports your head, or lie down. A quiet spot is helpful, but you don't have to go into a soundproof booth.
2. Next, put one hand on your upper chest and the other hand on your abdomen. Breathe as you normally do. Notice which hand moves the most as you breathe. Don't change your breathing.
3. Which hand moves the most? The top one? High, shallow, chest breathing is physiologically connected with the go mode. Low, deep, belly breathing is physiologically connected with the rest mode.
4. Now put both hands on your lower abdomen. Breathe by expanding and contracting your belly to allow the breath to come in and out. Imagine you have a balloon in your stomach, and it is going to fill and empty as your belly rises and falls.
5. Breathe in—any old way—then contract your belly to exhale. Pull those tummy muscles in toward your lower back as if you're blowing out those 39 candles on your birthday cake.

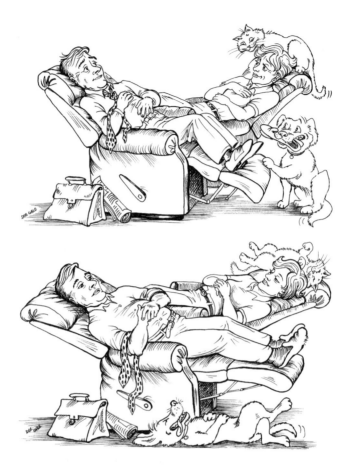

6. Then, let your belly rise, and the air will come in naturally.
7. Gently pull in your tummy muscles again to exhale. Let your belly rise as the air comes in.
8. You are not forcing the breath, not breathing more quickly. It's an easy, natural rhythm, like a swinging gate.

This is how you used to breathe as a baby. With practise, it can again become your natural way of breathing. Do this for a few minutes to get used to how it feels.

7. Enjoy the Relax/Recharge

You can do this after your relaxation breathing for more R and R. You may get so relaxed you go to sleep—that's okay. Or you may get so agitated you leap up to watch TV—that's okay, too.

1. Gently, tighten the muscles of your face. Feel the tension. Breathe in. Then as you exhale, let go. Release any tension in your face. Let the muscles of your face be relaxed. Your forehead, eyes, jaw and mouth relax. Your expression becomes soft. Let go a little more each time you exhale.

2. Make fists with your hands and tighten your arms. Gently push your fists against the chair. Feel the tension. Breathe in. As you exhale, let your neck, shoulders and arms relax. Let go a little more each time you exhale.

3. Tighten your thighs and buttocks, and push down with your heels. Press your legs against the chair. Breathe in. As you exhale, let go of any tension. Let go a little more each time you exhale.

4. Now focus your attention on your breathing. Feel the movement of your breath. Don't force your breathing, but imagine your tension going out as you exhale. Let go a little more each time you exhale.

5. Sit quietly for a few minutes. Your attention is lightly focused on your breathing, and you are letting go with each exhalation. If other thoughts intrude, gently bring your mind back to your breathing. Thoughts will come up—let them come and let them go. Keep coming back to the movement of your breathing.

6. Enjoy this quiet feeling of ease. Enjoy the health-giving benefits recharging every cell.

You may hear an inner voice chastise, "You're wasting time. Get on with things." Nagging is neither helpful nor accurate—this is time well spent.

It is very helpful to do this each day, for ten minutes: a good time to do this is after work, or before you go to sleep at night. As you practise, it will get easier.

I have developed a relax/recharge cassette tape for Type A's. This tape is designed to help you learn and enjoy belly breathing, muscle relaxation, hand warming, and mindfulness meditation. (To order, please see the back of the book.)

8. Practise Hand Warming

Here is another technique from my program. This one is based on Autogenic Training, a system where the mind directs various parts of the body with suggestive phrases to, for example, relax muscles or increase blood flow to the extremities. This technique is often used with biofeedback in the treatment of hypertension, migraine and other vascular conditions. It was developed by physicians Johannes Schultz and Wolfgang Luthe.

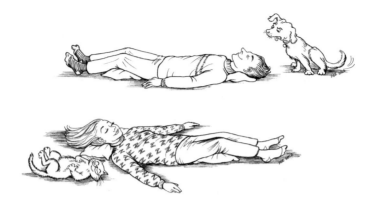

1. Lie down or sit in a comfortable chair that supports your head.
2. Do a few minutes of belly breathing until you slow down and settle in.
3. Then repeat these phrases to yourself.

    My arms and hands are heavy.
    My arms and hands are heavy and warm.
    My arms and hands are letting go.
    My whole body is letting go.
    As I relax, my stress gauge is coming down.
    My legs and feet are heavy.
    My legs and feet are heavy and warm.
    My legs and feet are letting go.
    My whole body is letting go.
    As I relax, my stress gauge is coming down.
    As I relax, my fuel gauge is going up.

Repeat this three times, letting go more each time.

9. Try the Relaxation Space Technique

This technique, based on a Zen meditation exercise, was developed by Eugene Gendlin and then refined by Dr. Les Fehmi, who calls it "Open Focus."

1. To begin, sit comfortably in a chair, or stretch out on a sofa. Imagine your head is filled with space. Imagine your eyes are filled with space. Your forehead. Your nose. Your mouth. Your jaw.
2. Imagine your torso is filled with space. Be aware of the space between the front of your chest and your back. Between your shoulders. In your tummy. In your buttocks. Feel the volume of this area. The area is filled with space.

3. Imagine your arms and hands are filled with space. (If you really want to get into this, go through the body bit by bit—each finger, each toe, and so on.) Imagine your legs and feet are filled with space. Feel the volume within your legs, within your feet. All is filled with space.

4. Visualize your fuel gauge filling up with fresh, life-giving energy. Look to your dashboard now. Your stress gauge is lower. Your fuel gauge is higher. Your temperature gauge is normal. Your speedometer is way down. Your blood pressure is lower. Your energy is higher. Your digestion is normal. The effect is stunning.

This technique is very effective at accessing the right hemisphere of the brain, a process that in itself is very relaxing. Another good way to shift into your right brain is to look off into the distance—look out into the sky.

10. Use Relaxation in Action—Being On-the-Spot

Reflect for a moment what your stress gauge would be like if you turned some of those time-wasting tortures, such as queuing at the bank, into opportunities to recharge. Outrageous? Yes! But why not? You know what to do now when you're stuck in traffic—talk yourself down and do a few moments of belly breathing.

When Type A's tell me they have no time to relax or recharge, I ask them to catch these moments, gear down and refuel:

- While caught in slow traffic
- While waiting for slow people
- While on hold during a telephone call
- While waiting for the elevator
- While waiting for a delayed flight at the airport
- While waiting for your ride, which is late
- While waiting for the show to begin at the movie theatre

Look for valuable opportunities everywhere—even in the elevator, when you're waiting for your floor. (No need to lean on the Door Close button now; just take the extra millisecond to bathe your system in relaxation hormones.) I bet you can easily find 30 minutes a day in your busy schedule to gear down.

11. Repeat Positive Self-Talk Often

Remember the stokers below the decks? Your nervous system reacts to what it hears from your brain. You fly around the office moaning, "I can't get all this done. It's too much. I have to do this. And then this." (This self-torture usually takes place at night in bed; you toss and turn, agonizing over this endless list, and you can't do anything about any of it.) This is anxious self-talk.

Your nervous system reacts much differently when you change your mantra to, "I'll do what I can do." This signals you are in control. Every cell of your body reacts differently. Even your immune system reacts positively.

The Healthy Type A self-talk sounds like this:

Situation: You face an approaching deadline.
Positive Self-Talk: "Let's prioritize. Item One is the most important; it has to be done by ———. Item Two can be done later. We can do it."

Situation: You are late for an appointment. The traffic just won't move.
Positive Self-Talk: "Well, it looks as if I'm going to be late. I don't like being late, but there's not much I can do about it. I'll explain when I get there. I'm confident that this won't sour the deal. This is a great opportunity for me to unwind."

Situation: You're standing at the hand dryer in the washroom.
Positive Self-Talk: "Ah, yes. This takes a whole minute. I can catch my breath."

This technique probably sounds simplistic to you. Well, it is, but it works. When I was counselling Kim, she queried whether just taking a moment to breathe and gear down (when she noticed her stress cue) was going to be enough. No, I said, not by itself. But breathing more deeply is an important component of the program. As she soon learned, Step 1 of this program is very helpful. Kim gained more insight into how much of her pressure was self-imposed and how one-sided her life had become. And she made a conscious effort to bring soul-restoring self-expression, in the form of water-colour painting, into her life.

I could feel the emotion in her voice when she told me, "I have always really enjoyed painting, but before the paint dried my critical side used to lash out at me. I would tear up the paper and throw it away. Now, I try not to pay any attention to that voice. I'm easing up on myself. After all, I'm not trying to be a professional; I'm just trying to have some fun. Now I can."

12. Slow Down

The main point of this technique is simply to slow down. Make an effort to talk a bit slower, walk a bit slower, eat a bit slower and drive a bit slower; if you do, you might even live longer. The belly breathing is the answer here. Slowing down will make it much easier to see what you're doing as you're doing it. I'm not asking you to dawdle; there's no need to fall into the other extreme. I'm just recommending that you try to find a balance in whatever you do.

As Marie, one of my former group participants, said, "Just making a conscious effort to slow down made a big difference. I began to notice so much more. As a result, I was able to change my reactions as I was in the midst of something. My old habit was to feel awful *after* an outburst—when it was too late. Now, I catch myself *before* I overreact. My cue is hunching my shoulders. Whenever I feel them go up, I automatically gear down. It works."

13. Reduce Caffeine

How are you doing with Step 2? If you are cutting back on caffeine, do it gradually to avoid a withdrawal headache. You may feel a little more tired as your body adapts. Breathe more deeply and get outside for some fresh air. Hang in there. This is really worth the effort. Ask for that *latte* decaf and experiment with no-caffeine drinks. A favourite of mine is spring water and white grape juice: there's no added sugar, no colouring, no caffeine.

14. Reduce Phone Stress

Set aside a time period to receive and make calls. At other times, let your machine answer. Make that deal and arrange that appointment, but come down a few pegs so your stress gauge is at 50 instead of 70. You can relax the muscles in your neck, in your shoulders, in your lower back, as you chatter away. You can be relaxed even when you're engaged in conversation.

15. Create Some Energy

The more you slump in your chair, the more tired you become. In this position, your blood and your brain lack oxygen. The fluids of your lymph system and your life-force energy stagnate, get sludgy. This causes more fatigue, which is a factor in depression, chronic pain and ill health. (See Step 9, to get things flowing again.) When you hear yourself complain about being tired, get out for a brisk walk—not to burn calories but to recharge.

16. Fill Your Mind with Happiness

When my mind is filled with fatigue or frustration, I take myself to the local recreation centre, soak in the hot tub and then do a few laps in the pool. I am not an exercise fanatic, but when my fuel gauge is low, I go for a good walk or swim, or I jump up and down (like a fool) to old Beatles tunes. During these activities, endorphins flood my system. The blood and *chi* flow. My right brain engages, and I'm more in touch with my body. All these processes fill my mind with happiness. Everyone can do this.

17. Create Some Space

When you have been beating your head against a wall in frustration, go and do something different. "But I'm just about done," you keep saying. An hour later, you are even more of a wreck. If you've been feeling stuck, struggling with something too long, you're going to do a much better job if you put it aside and come back to it later. Let it go. Create some psychological space. Go for a walk. Expand your horizons. Watch the clouds in the sky. This break will balance your brain and rest your eyes.

18. Create Some Fun

Put something fun on your list of Things To Do. Make this a priority. Dig out that sketch-book, that guitar or those bird-watching binoculars that used to be a source of creative pleasure. So many overworked people lament, "I used to love to sing. I used to dabble in poetry. I used to love to read novels on rainy days." And they promise themselves, "When the kids are grown, when we retire . . . then we will do the things we enjoy." My friends, that day may never come. Live your life more fully now.

Recently, my usually very busy husband, a landscaper, came home in the middle of a bright sunny day and asked me if I'd like to go for a walk on the beach. I said of course, but wondered what had inspired him.

He explained, "One of my clients pleaded with me today, 'Don't make the same mistake my husband and I made. We worked very hard all our lives, saying we would enjoy life when we retired. He died before that happened. Go home and take your wife to the beach.' So let's go." And we did.

19. Create Some Connection

Overloaded stress disconnects your body and mind. You may even walk with your head leaning out over your feet. Or you might find yourself in the shower, completely lost in your thoughts, look down and be surprised to see your body standing there. This is what is meant by being stuck "in your head."

One of the hallmarks of the unhealthy Type A is this dominance of the mind over the heart and the body. Like a dictator, the forceful mind will override symptoms that are trying to serve as wake-up calls and push your body to the max. (This tyrant can even keep you from going to the bathroom when you're busy. This is very hard on your bladder and your bowels.)

This dominance and imbalance are exacerbated if you are also left-brain dominant. Getting back into your body—feeling the synchronization of body and mind—is very helpful. T'ai chi, yoga and gentle stretching are wonderful for this. Meditation is also very good. (See more in Step 9.)

20. Create Some Love and Colour

People who form warm social bonds are usually healthier and live longer. Reconnecting with your loved ones can uncoil that inner tightness. Open up and share your current struggle with a friend. If you truly speak from the heart, it will bring you and your friend closer.

As Marie's awareness increased, she realized how her overcrowded life lacked colour and emotional nourishment. She made a conscious effort to contact friends with whom she had lost touch. Kim had never really had close friends, and although she was certainly a go-getter Type A, she was also quite shy. It was an effort for her to open up to others, but she did it and found this enriched her life and reduced her stress.

If you find intimacy difficult, look to your early conditioning. Were you taught to keep your feelings hidden inside? Were you taught to equate vulnerability with weakness? If so, you may fear being close to someone. Part of you may want companionship and love; the other side may hold back. Look at how this may be a factor in keeping you from giving and receiving the love that is all around. Were emotional upheavals strongly discouraged in your family? If so, you're missing a lot of what it is to be human. Our emotions have all sorts of wonderful colours.

In some cultures, singing and loving and dancing are seen as essentials—they are what it means to be alive. If your life is monochromatic, you may feel grey inside. What can you do to spice up your life? To bring more joie de vivre into it? Perhaps, go out for dinner to a lively Italian restaurant, wear something red, sip some good wine, savour each morsel of your meal. Really listen to the happy sounds around you. Feel as if you have not a care in the world. Let go and laugh.

Ask your companion questions about his or her heart's desires. Really listen to what your friend has to say. Step out of your cocoon and reveal a bit more of yourself. Feel how good it is to relate with another person on a meaningful level—beyond the weather, the dollar, the demands of your life. Living your life more fully is within your reach.

21. Create Some Down Time to Recharge Your Batteries

Sometimes it's good to be quiet. To be by yourself. To watch the birds soaring overhead. To savour the soft colours of the landscape, the vivid colours of the sky. To read an absorbing book that has nothing to do with work and that makes your heart and soul sing.

Not too long ago I had a week of doing nothing. No, this is not another form of torture. For the healthy A, this is a Type A delight.

I was on a mountain-top retreat. Away from the phone. Away from the fax. Away from having to keep all those spinning plates in the air.

Now as I sit writing this, fresh creative energy and renewed inspiration surge through my system. My inner resources are restocked. There's a feeling of quiet strength and confidence that I can deal with whatever comes up. A feeling of ease. I have the patience to tackle the ongoing queue of demands. The "need attention" papers are still piled high on my desk, but there's more space in my mind. (This is different than being "spaced out.")

Nothing would make me happier than for you to put down this book now, pick up the phone and make plans for a nature getaway. If you're feeling burnt out, depressed or agitated much of the time, a retreat from the flurry of everyday demands is crucial. Take this book with you to help you unwind and rejuvenate. You *can* turn your life around. This may take some fiddling with your schedule, but it's well worth the effort.

Let's look at some R and R options:

Out of town: call your travel agent for suggestions. Consider an ocean cruise, a quiet beach or a resort spa. If you can squeeze this out of your budget once a year, it's well worth it. (One of my friends takes her lunch to work and forgoes eating out throughout the year. With the money she saves, she goes to Mexico for two weeks each winter. And she eats healthier food by preparing her own meals.)

In town: I bet there are hotels with spa facilities near where you live, with all the benefits of being away without the travel. Even a few days can be enough to boost your worn-out batteries. Leave the phone number of the spa at home, with strict instructions that its use is for emergencies only.

At home: this is a challenge, but possible. You'll need to set boundaries. Not answering the phone is a good start. Keep away from watching TV every day. Get a stack of old videos that make you laugh or make you feel uplifted. Move into the guest room, if you have one. Listen to some relaxing music. Get some good books and make a fresh fruit plate to nibble from while you read. You may feel really exhausted at first. This is your system taking advantage of the break to heal itself. Hang in there; soon your energy will rise again.

You can always go for a swim at your local recreation centre and soak in the hot tub. Take a yoga or t'ai chi class. Learn to meditate (see Step 9). Possibilities abound.

22. Take Regular Down Time

Many powerful people who are able to stay the distance with the plate game take a quick power snooze some time during the day. This refreshes your brain, which can operate for only a limited time at a stretch. Much better than caffeine, a short power nap is a marvellous way to refuel.

There's a Calvin and Hobbes cartoon in which Calvin is gleefully jumping about outside. His dad passes by and extols "the significant cardio-vascular benefits of such activity." Calvin suddenly looks glum and uninterested. Do you, like Calvin, react negatively to something that's supposed to be good for you?

When I try to teach go-getters how to relax and recharge, invariably some hard-core cases announce that they relax, just fine, thank you very much—playing hard-hitting tennis or jogging until they drop.

I wonder if they even cool down afterwards or if they dash in and out of the shower, leap into their clothes, jump into the car and soon land in the midst of the office whirlwind. These Type A's would be much healthier if they took ten minutes of down time afterwards.

23. Try Doing Nothing

One of the best ways to recharge is to sit still and do nothing. Another Type A Torture, you say. By *doing nothing*, I mean allowing your mind and body to slow down. Try actually sitting in that garden chair you usually mow around. Let your neck and shoulders relax. Let your breathing become slower and deeper. Let go of the tension as you exhale. Ignore the voice that tries to make you feel guilty for doing nothing. You are doing something very worthwhile. Enjoy this simple act of settling into stillness.

Focus your attention on the sights, sounds and smells around you. Tune in to the moment. Be where you are.

In a few moments, you may long to leap into action. "What about those weeds!" you say and scurry off for the weed killer. And the hedge needs trimming. And the barbecue needs cleaning. And on and on you go. Doing things is great, but it is essential to balance activity with rest.

24. Create Some Connection to the Sacred World

Being in nature is essential for your soul. There are natural energies all around us; the Japanese call them *kami*, the Tibetans call them *dralas*, Aboriginal people call them part of the Great Spirit. Stand beside a cascading waterfall or beside an ancient cedar tree, and tune in to what you feel. Stroll along a beach beside the pounding surf. Tune in. What do you feel? Do you feel the same as when you stand in an underground parking lot? Or do you experience something else?

Our culture doesn't have a name for these natural energies because the concrete cocoons that we work and live in disconnect us from each other and from the earth on which we stand. We do not even acknowledge these energies. Make these nature getaways a priority. Enjoy them. Tell that city slave driver voice of yours that this is time well spent. Stepping outside of your everyday routine into a larger, fresher world gives you greater perspective—and it's fun.

25. Create Some Deeper Purpose

Invigorate your sense of purpose by finding deeper meaning in your life. Find out what you can do to contribute to the greater good. First, you have to discover your passion; then employ your talents to do something. We A's have so much that we can give to make this a better world. Making a contribution to your community, by volunteering your time where it's needed, is an expression of "conscious living." Helping others can be richly rewarding and make you appreciate what you have, all the more. And it will ease your stress, too.

Some of My Own Medicine

Recently, I gave three important packages to my cross-town courier. My instructions were explicit: even though the parcels looked the same, it was important that the driver made sure each went to the proper person. Sure enough, two people called me complaining they had received the wrong one. I called the courier company. I was a bit overheated, I'll admit, but they'd mucked up orders before. The manager listened patiently, then asked, "Is that Dr. Crofton?"

"Ah, yes," I replied.

"Well, I took one of your stress seminars. I suggest you take a deep breath and relax."

11-5   © 1974 Jim Unger

**"I thought your doctor told you
to get away and RELAX."**

STEP 5

Take Stock of Your Health

If you're not concerned about suddenly finding yourself with a serious heart disease or cancer, wake up!... You have the opportunity to take control over many of the risk factors of premature death. Alcohol, tobacco and poor nutrition don't have to kill you. You can take steps now to help you live a long, vigorous life, staying healthy and active well into your 80s and even 90s.

Elliott J. Howard, M.D.
Health Risks

**"Another day, another chance something
will be found hazardous to my health"**

Ever feel like this? The basic rule of thumb seems to be if it tastes good and feels good it's probably bad for you. Now, is that fair? While we're all interested in our health, sometimes we get a little fed up. Like this poor fellow, Fred. His wife used to berate him mercilessly about the fried eggs, bacon, buttered white toast and coffee he loved. He is instead about to tuck into an oat-bran-and-skim-milk breakfast.

She's not trying to make his life miserable; she's just trying to keep her husband alive. But sometimes her nagging is too much. (A scolding tone of voice immediately creates resistance.) In defiance, Fred sneaks out of bed in the middle of the night to raid the fridge. And he doesn't see that the choices he keeps making are draining the health gauge on his dashboard and increasing his risk of illness.

How healthy do you want to be? And for how many years?

The health gauge reflects your storehouse of health reserves. It's like a bank account. And no matter how big your overdraft allowance, every once in a while you've got to make a deposit.

Most of us start off with a full account of good health. But, as we get older and use up our reserves, we become more susceptible to illness and injury. As we age, our system has had to filter stress hormones, booze, nicotine, fatty foods, preservatives, pesticides and pollution. This accumulation depletes our health account.

Not too long ago I went to watch an "old boys'" rugby match. Grey-haired guys ran down the field; their big bellies protruded, stretching the stripes on their shirts. At half-time, the scene looked like a battlefield: all these injured heaps lying with ice packs on their strained muscles. (I wanted to advise them that a "bowling ball belly" increases their risk of a heart attack significantly—more than carrying weight in other places.)

In this vital step of my program, we A's decide to pause long enough to take stock of our health and assess our longevity and risk of heart disease, cancer and immune-related illnesses. Not only do we want to learn how to boost our batteries, but we want to be around for many years to come and in good shape.

As we go through this, I'll try my best not to be the scolding parent, and you can try your best not to be the rebellious child. I just want you to make informed choices. Too many A's die younger than their Type B counterparts, from ignorance, or, at least, from ignoring.

The real challenge for a health educator like me is to get people, like you, motivated before a crisis. Because you've made it to Step 5, I presume you already realize this, but, as you know, some folks rationalize, "You can't live forever." If they want to go out in a blaze of glory early, that's their choice. Or is it?

This questionnaire gives a rough measure of longevity.

Circle the score for each characteristic that applies to you. Some may add to your score; some may subtract from it. Then total the score and check your risk category.

Take This Test to Measure Your Longevity

Family History
Choose any that apply.

−2 Both mother and father were free of cancer and heart disease and lived beyond age 75

−1 Only one parent was free of cancer and heart disease and lived beyond 75

+2 Coronary heart disease before age 50 in one or both parents

+3 Coronary heart disease before age 40 in one or both parents

+2 High blood pressure before age 50 in only one parent

+3 High blood pressure before age 50 in both parents

+1 Diabetes mellitus before age 60 in one or both parents

+2 Cancer in a parent or sibling

+2 Stroke before age 60 in only one parent

+3 Stroke before age 60 in both parents

Weight
Choose one.

 0 Normal or within 10% of normal

+2 Overweight by 20–29%

+3 Overweight by 30–39%

+4 More than 40% overweight

Blood Pressure (in mm)

Systolic	*Diastolic*
Choose one.	Choose one.
−1 100–120	−1 60–70
0 121–140	0 71–85
+1 141–170	+1 86–100
+2 171–190	+2 101–110
+3 Over 190	+3 111–120
	+4 Over 120

Cholesterol (in mL)

Total	*HDL*
Choose one.	Choose one.
−2 3.9–4.3	−2 1.7–2.1
−1 4.4–4.9	−1 1.3–1.7
0 5.0–5.4	0 1.1–1.3
+1 5.5–6.2	+1 0.8–1.0
+2 6.3–7.2	+2 0.6–0.7
+3 7.3–8.3	+3 below 0.6
+4 Over 8.3	

Smoking

Choose any that apply.

−1 Never smoked

−1 Quit over 5 years ago

 0 Quit 1 to 5 years ago

+1 Quit within the past year

+2 Smoke less than 1 pack of cigarettes a day

+3 Smoke 1 pack of cigarettes a day

+4 Smoke about 1½ packs of cigarettes a day

+5 Smoke 2 packs of cigarettes a day

+1 Smoke a pipe or cigars

+3 Began smoking as a teenager

+5 Have smoked for more than 20 years

+1 Smoke marijuana 1 or 2 times a week

+2 Smoke marijuana daily

+1 Live *or* work in heavily air-polluted area

+2 Live *and* work in heavily air-polluted area

Alcohol Use

Choose any that apply.

−1 Drink no more than 1½ ounces of hard liquor, 12 ounces of beer or 5 ounces of wine once or twice a week

 0 Drink almost every day but not more than 1½ ounces of hard liquor, 12 ounces of beer or 5 ounces of wine a day

+1 Drink two drinks each day totalling 3 ounces of hard liquor, 24 ounces of beer or 10 ounces of wine

+2 Drink more than two drinks each day

+5 Smoke cigarettes, pipe or cigar, and drink alcohol at least several times a week

Personality and Stress Evaluation
Choose any that apply.
+1 Intense desire to get ahead
+2 Constant driving need for success
+2 Easily irritated, annoyed or frustrated
+2 Angry and hostile if losing in competition
+2 Fiercely competitive; must win
+3 Angry and hostile, even if successful
+1 Have many projects going on at once
+1 Constantly bothered by incomplete work
+2 Don't express anger; hold feelings inside
+2 Work hard without feeling satisfaction
+2 Frequent stress symptoms—knot in stomach, heart palpitations, headaches, poor sleep, intestinal symptoms, constipation
+2 Hardly laugh; depressed often
+2 Rarely discuss problems or feelings with others
+2 Constantly strive to please others rather than yourself
−1 None of the above

Exercise
Choose one in each group, then calculate your score for this section as indicated at the end of this section.
Frequency of Exercise
+5 Daily or almost daily
+4 3–5 times a week
+3 1–2 times a week
+2 2–3 times a month
+1 Less than 3 times a month
Duration of Each Exercise Period
+4 More than 45 minutes
+3 20–40 minutes
+2 10–20 minutes
+1 Less than 10 minutes
Intensity of Each Exercise Period
+5 Sustained vigorous exercise

+4 Intermittent vigorous exercise

+3 Moderately vigorous exercise

+2 Moderately non-vigorous exercise

+1 Light, leisurely activity

To determine your fitness rating, multiply your score for each section.

_____X_____X_____=_____
   Intensity   Duration   Frequency   Score

For example: 3 x 4 x 3 = 36. The maximum is 100. Use your answer to determine your physical fitness rating below.

Physical Fitness Rating

Choose one.

−2 81–100 is very active, high fitness

−1 61–80 is active and healthy

  0 41– 60 is acceptable and good

+1 31–40 is not good enough

+2 21–30 is inadequate

+3 20 and below is sedentary, poor fitness

Dietary Habits

Choose any that apply.

+2 Use salt freely, without tasting food first

+2 Eat cabbage, broccoli or cauliflower less than 3 times a week

+3 Eat high-fibre grains, such as whole wheat bread, brown rice and bran cereal, less than once a day

+3 Eat fewer than 3 fruits and vegetables a day

+1 Follow a fad weight-loss diet once or twice a year

Eat heartily at meals, and snack between meals:

+3 Daily or almost daily

+2 4 days a week

+1 2 days a week

Eat beef, bacon or processed meats:

+3 5–6 times a week

+2 4 times a week

+1 2 times a week

Eat eggs, alone or in other foods:

+3 12 eggs a week

+2 8 eggs a week

+1 6 eggs a week

Eat ice cream, cake or rich desserts:

+2 Almost every day

+1 Several times a week

Eat butter, cream, cream cheese and cheese:

+3 Every day

+2 Almost every day

+1 2–3 times a week

Sex and Physical Build

Choose one.

 0 Male, with slim build

+1 Male, heavily muscled, with stocky build

+3 Female, take birth control pills and smoke

+1 Female, post-menopausal and take estrogen

 0 Female, take birth control pills and don't smoke

 0 Female, post-menopausal and don't take estrogen

Interpreting Your Score

To determine your score, add all scores from the categories. Check your total score below to see if your health and your life are at risk.

−15   *Lowest Risk*—This is the best possible score. You should enjoy a long, healthy life free of cancer, heart disease, stroke or diabetes.

−14 to +6   *Low Risk*—You are in very good health; odds are in your favour of continued good health and a long, productive life free of cancer, heart disease, diabetes and stroke. If you wish to improve your odds, check the test to see where you gained points. If possible, work on improving those areas.

7 to 11   *Moderate Risk*—You are at some risk of developing ill-health and can expect to live an average life span. Try to correct conditions or habits for which you scored a 2, 3 or 4, and you may help add years to your life.

12 to 20   *High Risk*—Your risk of developing a life-threatening illness early in life and dying sooner than you should is considerable.

You can help lower your risk by correcting conditions for which you scored a 2, 3 or 4.

21+   *Very High Risk*—Your health is at dangerous risk, and you may die prematurely if you don't change your ways immediately to begin to correct your unhealthy habits. Seek professional advice to help you quit smoking, improve your diet and/or begin an exercise plan.

Source: Reprinted by kind permission of Elliott J. Howard, M.D.

A Close Call Can Wake Us Up

Some people are just too busy to fill out questionnaires. Like Kirk. Remember him? He is the enslaved go-getter, introduced in Step 3, who finds it difficult to pace himself. Convinced of his immortality, he sees no need to take stock of his health and doesn't realize he is at risk of losing his health—and his marriage.

Increasingly louder alarm bells fail to warn him. If we could catch him on the run and ask if his health and his marriage are important to him, he would answer curtly, over his shoulder, "Of course." But based on how he allocates his time, neither appears to be a priority. Kirk is lucky, however. He is going to get two close calls that will wake him up. With a jolt.

Over the years, Kirk's wife, Beverly, has grown increasingly impatient with his workaholism. Even when pressed into going out for dinner with her, he is distracted and either doesn't talk much or goes on and on about the falling dollar or rising interest rates. When they get home, he darts into his office, saying he has "to make a few quick calls before bed." *Some* date.

This situation reaches a head, one Saturday night. The dinner guests are expected in 15 minutes. Beverly has been cooking feverishly for hours. She calls out to Kirk to set the table. Somehow between hearing her request and finishing the task, he remembers he must call his accountant. He dashes into his office to make a quick, and hopefully unnoticed, call. (Why the accountant is available at that hour is another story.)

As usual, the call goes on longer than he expected.

Beverly is putting the last touches on the meal. She hears the doorbell, and when Kirk doesn't answer, she goes to greet the guests. When she brings them in and sees that the table isn't set, she has finally taken all she can. For the sake of their friends she tries to contain herself during the dinner, but later she tells Kirk that their marriage is over.

He is stunned. Completely stunned. How could she act so impulsively? So irrationally? Doesn't she appreciate how tough it is out there and that he's doing all this for her and for the kids? All she knows is that she can't—doesn't want to—take it any more. After many heated discussions, Kirk moves out.

Pushing harder than ever to escape the pain gnawing at him, he's a wreck. "No, I'm fine," he states to anyone foolish enough to ask. "I'm just fine." Revealing emotion to himself or to anyone else has always been verboten in his family.

His blood pressure is higher and he is sometimes short of breath. "Nothing to worry about. Happens to lots of people." Kirk smokes, but he is going to quit, "as soon as things slow down." He has a tool-box of very effective, socially acceptable uppers and downers: caffeine and scotch. "I believe in enjoying life," he tells anyone who looks askance. Kirk has taken up smoking expensive cigars. This makes him feel like a big shot.

One night he wakes up with a crushing pain in his chest. Nothing he tries seems to work. He feels nauseous and is in a cold sweat. "I'm fine," he tries to reassure himself. "Just indigestion." The squeezing pain becomes more severe. Like a bolt from the blue, it hits him. He is having a heart attack. "How could this be? This couldn't happen to me. Not to me. I'm too young."

He manages to get himself dressed, grabs the keys and gets into the car. Somehow he makes it to the hospital but suddenly slumps over the wheel. Fortunately, the night guard sees him, and two paramedics quickly carry him into the emergency room.

Kirk has done many stupid things, but this is the most stupid, as far as his life is concerned. Even a non-smoker having a heart attack has nearly a 50 percent chance of dying in the first hour, and, as a smoker, his chances of sudden death are four times greater. Calling 911 instead of driving could have made the difference between life and death. (Not just his, either; think of the fate of another driver or a poor pedestrian in his path if he lost consciousness while driving.)

Thanks to the emergency room staff he lives through the night. The next day, a stern-looking cardiologist turns out to be harder on him than his wife ever was. The straight-talking doctor refuses to take Kirk on as a patient if he continues to smoke. Kirk is indignant but acquiesces, fear being a surprisingly strong motivator. Having to give up smoking is not the only insult to his much-cherished independence. He has to give up the fast foods he relishes. He thought he'd finished stripping his life of all its pleasures when "Doctor Killjoy," as Kirk refers to him behind his back, starts in about alcohol and the heart, then stress and the heart. Enough already!

Kirk misses his family. Lying in his hospital bed, gazing out at the expanse of blue sky, he feels a wave of emotion wash over him. He realizes how much his family means to him. He calls Beverly to see if they can get together.

"It's no good. You don't listen. To me or to your doctors," Beverly protests.

"I do now!" asserts Kirk. He tells her about his recent escape.

Beverly is shocked but recovers enough to consider his offer.

"We'll talk about it later, when you're better."

"No, I want to talk about it now." Kirk hasn't lost *all* his impatience.

"All right," Beverly replies, "But if we were to get back together, you would have to let some things go."

"I can't let *everything* go," Kirk protests.

Beverly continues, "You don't have to. Just learn to say no, once in awhile. Let your staff take more responsibility. Leave your briefcase at the office some evenings and spend more time with your family."

He seems to be listening, so she continues, "The kids hardly ever see you. And when they do, you're exhausted. I don't want our family to break up, but I can't go back to living the way we used to."

"I'm different now. You'll see. Will you give me one more chance?" Kirk is truly speaking from his heart. Somehow the attack has opened him up.

Beverly softens. "I'm willing to give it a try. Why don't we get out of town for a weekend when you're well enough. Think you would be able to leave your beloved pager at home?"

He feels a moment of panic, which surprises him. Has he really become so enslaved to that thing?

"Hey, what does it matter if I miss a few calls on a weekend? I can catch them the next week. No problem."

It's Beverly's turn to be stunned. Maybe he *has* changed.

Taking charge of his health proves to be easier than Kirk had feared. After such a close call, he is glad to be alive and promises himself that he isn't going to waste this second chance. He resolves to stop fighting the clock and start fighting for the things that he now realizes are the most important to him.

He still loves his work, but it no longer rules his life. To his great surprise his business continues to do well. He has learned to set limits and to say no more often. He now sees the value in letting his staff take some of the load and is surprised at how well they do. They even got along without him while he was in hospital! He makes time to give them the information and coaching they need. He's enjoying the shift from the do-it-all-myself work hog, to the let's-work-together, encouraging coach.

He has cut back on alcohol and caffeine and has signed up for a stop-smoking program at the YMCA. Every evening he takes 15 minutes of down time when he gets home from work. After that he has enough energy to throw a ball around outside with his children.

For too many of us, it takes a brush with death, a divorce or some other crisis to wake us up.

My friends, please, if you get nothing else out of this book, take stock of your health now. Do you know your blood pressure? Your cholesterol level? Your risk of having a heart attack? If you are old enough to remember watching Ed Sullivan on TV, you need to know these things.

If your heart could speak to you, what would it say? Please find out. Your well-being and perhaps your life are at stake.

And if you're worried about a loved one, please don't nag. Instead, express your love and concern. Encourage him or her to fill out the questionnaires on pages 79 to 84; do it together. Make an appointment for both of you to get your blood pressure and cholesterol levels taken.

Are You at Risk for a Heart Attack?

If you listed the people most likely to have a heart attack or stroke, you'd probably include the easily angered hot reactor in your office, the puffy-faced TV reporter with the big belly and your chain-smoking neighbour. All likely candidates, perhaps.

Did you include yourself? "Surely not," you say. You are a hardy Type A: you never get sick, you're at your normal weight, you don't smoke, your blood pressure is fine or you are a woman. None of these alone will save you. What if you don't have any symptoms? Unfortunately, this doesn't count you out either. The first sign of trouble can be a fatal heart attack.

All of us know someone "too young to die," whose life ended abruptly because of a heart attack. This is Canada's number one killer, striking more people than cancer, car accidents and AIDS combined. Women may worry more about breast cancer, but heart disease kills seven times as many women—38,000 a year—in Canada. These fatalities include our loved ones, our co-workers, our peers—many who were only beginning to enjoy the leisure time they deserved. And according to the leading researcher in this area, Dr. Redford Williams of Duke University, in North Carolina, Type A's who are chronically hostile, mistrustful, aggressive or cynical are four to five times more likely to have heart disease than are the more easygoing folks.

As with Kirk, a health crisis has a way of waking up the followers of the God of Wishful Thinking, those people who seem to be waiting for a medical bulletin that reports "Recent medical studies prove steak and martinis significantly lower the risk of a heart attack. And if you also smoke and drive everywhere instead of walking, you reduce that risk even further." We know, of course, this is absurd.

Sure, "we all have to go sometime," as Wishful Thinkers tell us, but is that going to be at 85 years old or at 58 years old? Much depends on the choices we make. Early deaths from heart disease are largely predictable, and, the good news is, largely preventable.

Not all of us should be worried about heart disease, but all of us should be aware of the risk. To find out your risk level, complete the following quiz.

The Heart Challenge Risk Test

If you've had a heart attack or surgery, you know where you stand. This is a quiz for those who don't know. It will give you a rough estimate of your heart attack risk. You can count on your fingers or keep score here.

1. You're a man over 45 — 1 finger _____
   A woman over 55 — 1 finger _____
2. You smoke more than a pack a day — 3 fingers _____
   Less than a pack — 2 fingers _____
   You're exposed to second hand smoke regularly — 1 finger _____
3. You do not make an effort to choose lower fat foods — 2 fingers _____
4. You've been told by a health professional that your blood cholesterol level is high — 2 fingers _____
5. You have diabetes — 2 fingers _____
6. You've been told by a health professional that your blood pressure is high — 2 fingers _____
7. You're substantially overweight — 2 fingers _____
   Moderately overweight — 1 finger _____
8. You're a couch potato — 2 fingers _____
9. You've been told that you should reduce the amount of stress in your life — 1 finger _____

10. One of your parents, a brother or sister had a heart
attack or stroke or bypass surgery before the age of 60 2 fingers _____

Your total score: _____

How did you rate?

0–3 fingers: lower risk.

4–7 fingers: moderate risk.

8 or more: higher risk.

This is only a subjective test, but if you scored in the moderate or high range, please check this out with your physician, soon. You might need medication, in addition to some lifestyle changes.

Managing Stress Cuts Your Heart Attack Risk

When I was working in that cardiac clinic in 1978, the connection between stress and heart disease was "inconclusive." Not any more. As the American Medical Association reported in 1997, "A stress-management program helped heart patients reduce their risk of heart attacks or the need for surgery by 74 percent. 'In addition to diet, quitting smoking and controlling blood pressure you need to think about managing stress,' said Dr. James Blumenthal, a professor of medical psychology at Duke University Medical Centre and the lead researcher of the study. Fifty to sixty percent of people with heart disease are believed to develop ischemia—impaired blood flow, which is known to worsen the out-look for heart patients—under mental stress."

Reduce Your High Blood Pressure

High blood pressure is often called the "silent killer" because it can be high enough to be fatal, without your knowing. The main risk factors are smoking, obesity, family history, a high-fat or high-salt diet, and excessive alcohol consumption. People with diabetes have an increased risk. High levels of caffeine may also contribute. And there's strong evidence that chronic high levels of stress can affect blood clotting, narrow and actually damage blood vessels and raise your cholesterol level.

Your heart works like a pump, sending blood, oxygen and nutrients around your body. If your blood vessels constrict due to smoking, stress or caffeine, your heart has to work much harder to push the blood around. Salt retains water, fat clogs and narrows the vessels, and obesity adds extra work—all of these increase your blood pressure.

Be sure to have your blood pressure checked. (And your blood fats—good and bad cholesterol and so on. All adults should know their levels. Then you know how seriously you need to take this information.)

You can, however, exert considerable control over your blood pressure. In many cases, lifestyle changes can reduce or even eliminate the need to take medication.

How to Reduce Your Blood Pressure without Drugs

- Eat less animal fat, and find a fitness activity that you enjoy to maintain a normal weight.
- Use herbs and spices to flavour your food instead of salt, and avoid canned foods, fast foods or frozen dinners with a high sodium content. Avoid salted chips and nuts.
- Cut back on alcohol and caffeine.
- Get into a stop-smoking program. High blood pressure and smoking can be a lethal combination.
- Practise the stress-reducing strategies and techniques in Step 4.

9-23   © 1978 Jim Unger

**"I'm well aware you're only 28 years old.
That's why I'm telling you to take
better care of yourself."**

Reducing the Risk of Cancer

The Healthy Type A Program had a big impact on Marie. When Marie began the program, her mother had already died of breast cancer and her older sister was in the midst of waging her own battle with the disease. With all Marie had been through, one would think Marie would have been vigilant about trying to protect herself against this disease. With such a family history, Marie's chance of being struck by breast cancer was very high—even higher than the one-in-nine risk most women face. Marie had a one-in-three risk of getting breast cancer. Yet, before she came to see me, she continued to smoke and eat a high-fat diet.

A gourmet with sophisticated tastes, Marie thought she ate light, but if we had followed her around with a fat gram counter, she would have been shocked by the results. For breakfast, she often had a croissant with her coffee and cream (flaky pastry has that texture because of lots of butter); lunch might be a cream soup with a shrimp Caesar salad (all high-fat choices). For dinner she often had salad with another high-fat dressing, chicken with the skin (because the skin was seasoned with fresh herbs) or pasta with garlic and cream sauce. For a snack, while watching television, she liked buttered popcorn and, sometimes before bed, a hot chocolate. She had a sweet tooth and was liable to treat herself, now and then, with deluxe ice cream or cheesecake.

Because of all the pressure in her life, Marie felt the need to drink alcohol, in the mistaken belief that it was a good way to relax. She did not think of herself as a drinker. But she was taking in quite a bit of alcohol in the few glasses of wine she had most nights. (An article in the *New England Journal of Medicine* has stated that consuming one alcoholic drink a day can significantly increase the potential for breast cancer.)

She wasn't smoking as much as she used to; this was one of her few concessions. But, as she lit up, what went through her mind? Marie is the kind of consumer who reads labels to avoid eating harmful preservatives and who drinks filtered water, yet as she dragged on her cigarette, she inhaled ammonia, formaldehyde, DDT (an insecticide) and thousands of other harmful chemicals.

Marie had begun smoking in her teens. Lighting up had made her feel chic. Would she have felt chic if she had been fully aware of inhaling so many poisons?

Marie told me that she had ignored her risk of cancer because dealing with it would have meant once again facing the heartbreak of her mother's death and the very real chance that she might meet the same fate.

What's Your Poison?

Most people know smoking is not healthy. What they don't know is that smoking is poisonous—for the smoker and for people who breathe second-hand smoke.

When you inhale tobacco smoke from your cigarette, or second-hand smoke, you breathe over 4,000 chemicals, including these poisons:

Acetone – Commonly used as a paint stripper.

Hydrogen Cyanide – Used in gas chambers.

Mercury, Lead and Cadmium – All three are toxic heavy metals. Mercury is the liquid used in thermometers. Lead and cadmium are found in car batteries.

Carbon Monoxide – The deadly, colourless, odourless gas in car exhaust.

DDT – An insecticide banned in Canada because of its harmful effects to the environment.

Formaldehyde – Used in funeral homes as embalming fluid and used as insulation in buildings.

Arsenic – Used as poison for pest control.

Nicotine – A drug, as addictive as heroin, that causes blood vessels to constrict and blood pressure to rise.

Source: Canadian Cancer Society

Breast cancer was not her only risk; Marie was also at risk for skin cancer. She went to Hawaii a few winters ago and lay on the beach soaking up the rays until she was a golden brown. She had been conditioned to see her tan as beautiful, not as something that ages and wrinkles her skin and significantly increases her risk of skin cancer.

Attaining optimum health is like playing a numbers game. To give ourselves a better shot at winning, we don't have to eliminate every risk; we need only improve our odds.

Take this test to measure your overall cancer risk. Circle the score for each characteristic that applies to you. Total the score, and then check your risk category at the end.

Rate Your Cancer Risk

Family History
Choose any that apply:
+2 One parent, aunt, uncle, grandparent or sibling with cancer

+15 More than one close relative with cancer

+10 One or more close relatives with cancer, *and* you smoke cigarettes, cigars or a pipe

+15 One or more close relatives with cancer, *and* you smoke, and drink more than one or two 5-ounce glasses of wine or 12-ounce glasses of beer, or 3 ounces of hard liquor a day, more than 5 days a week

+1 You drink more than 2 cups of caffeinated or decaffeinated coffee a day and have a close relative who had pancreatic cancer

Smoking
Choose any that apply:
+1 Smoke less than 1 pack of cigarettes a day

+5 Smoke 1 pack of cigarettes a day

+8 Smoke 2 or more packs of cigarettes a day

+10 Smoke 1 or more packs of cigarettes a day *and* drink two or three 5-ounce glasses of wine or 12-ounce glasses of beer, or 3 ounces of hard liquor a day, 5 or more days a week

+2 Smoke cigars or a pipe

+4 Smoke cigars or a pipe *and* drink two or three 5-ounce glasses of wine or 12-ounces glasses of beer, or 3 ounces of hard liquor a day, 5 or more days a week

+2 Live *or* work with smokers

+3 Live *and* work with smokers

+1 Live *or* work in heavily air-polluted area

+2 Live *and* work in heavily air-polluted area

Personal
Choose any that apply:
+8 Sunburn easily and have had one or more severe sunburns with peeling, blistering skin

+5 Do not tan easily and are exposed to strong sun only occasionally, such as during vacations or on weekends

+3 Overweight by 20 percent

+5 Overweight by 25 percent or more

+1 Have been overweight most of your life

+2 Known exposure to pesticides, toxic wastes or asbestos in air, water or soil

+3 Have had many diagnostic X-rays in your life, especially when young

+4 Drink more than three 5-ounce glasses of wine or 12-ounce glasses of beer, or 3 ounces of hard liquor a day, more than 5 days a week

+2 Lead a sedentary life without any regular, vigorous exercise

+1 Often feel lonely or isolated from other people

+1 Have no close friends or loved ones

+1 Feel depressed or overwhelmed much of the time

Diet

Choose any that apply:

−5 Do not eat meat

+1 Eat beef, pork and/or lamb 3 times a week

+2 Eat beef, pork and/or lamb 5 times a week

+3 Eat beef, pork and/or lamb more than 5 times a week

+2 Eat processed meats, such as bacon, bologna, sausage or ham twice a week

+3 Eat processed meats, such as bacon, bologna, sausage or ham 3 to 5 times a week

+4 Eat processed meats, such as bacon, bologna, sausage or ham more than 5 times a week

+2 Eat smoked or charcoal-grilled foods once a week

+1 Eat generous amounts of butter or margarine

+1 Eat fried foods several times a week

+2 Eat fried foods almost every day

+1 Eat rich desserts or ice cream several times a week

+2 Eat rich desserts or ice cream almost every day

+1 Drink at least 1 to 2 glasses of *whole* milk, or the equivalent, each day

+1 Eat cheese (except low-fat cottage cheese) several times a week

+2 Eat cheese (except low-fat cottage cheese) almost every day

+2 Eat empty-calorie foods or processed foods several times a week

+4 Eat empty-calorie foods or processed foods almost every day

+2 Eat less than two slices of whole-grain bread a day

+3 Eat high-fibre cereal less than 3 times a week

+3 Eat less than 3 servings of fresh fruits and vegetables a day

+3 Do not drink citrus juice or eat a citrus fruit every day

+3 Eat broccoli, cabbage, cauliflower or Brussels sprouts less than 3 times a week

Interpreting Your Score

To determine your score, add all scores from the categories. Check your total score below to see if your health and your life are at risk.

0–14   *Low Risk*—Your risk of cancer is low because you eat a proper diet, exercise and live a healthier lifestyle.

15–25   *Moderate Risk*—You have a moderate risk of developing cancer. To help lower your risk, follow a risk-reducing nutrition plan, stop smoking and begin an exercise program *now*.

26–35   *High Risk*—Your lifestyle is conspiring against you to raise your risk of cancer. Stop smoking now! Follow a risk-reducing nutrition plan and risk-reducing exercise plan, and you may significantly lower your risk.

36+   *Very High Risk*—Your family history and your unhealthy lifestyle are putting you at a very high risk of cancer. If you change your ways now, stop smoking, and begin a risk-reducing nutrition plan and risk-reducing exercise plan, you can help lower your risk considerably.

Source: Reprinted by kind permission of Elliott J. Howard, M.D.

It seems somewhat unfair that the foods we have grown up thinking of as healthy, such as meat, milk and cheese, may not be that good for us in normal to large quantities. However, we can enjoy eating some organic meats from animals raised without additives such as hormones and antibiotics. Beyond that, organic grains, fruits and vegetables, and high-quality nutritional supplements can significantly reduce our cancer risk (more on this in Steps 6 and 7).

How to Reduce Your Risk of Cancer

- Quit smoking altogether and stay away from second-hand smoke.
- If you are a woman, have regular check-ups with pap tests and breast exams—early detection is crucial. Also do a breast self-exam after every period.

- Cut down significantly on the fat in your diet, and eat more fresh fruit, vegetables and whole grains. A high-fibre diet reduces your risk of a number of cancers, including breast cancer.
- Cut down significantly on alcohol.
- Reduce the amount of stress in your life.
- Get into the routine of regular exercise. For women, being physically fit and at a healthy weight appears to help protect against breast cancer; women who have gained more than 20 pounds since their teenage years double their chances of getting breast cancer.
- Protect yourself against the cancer-causing rays of the sun. The skin cancer rates in sunny climes like Australia, California and Florida are astronomical. Melanoma can be fatal. Use a good sunscreen, avoid the harsh midday sun, wear a hat and retrain your brain to accept that a deep tan is not sexy. In my view, and many other people's, tanning salons should be shut down. They are not safer than outside tanning.
- Reduce your intake of additives and preservatives in food like nitrites, BHA and BHT. Read those labels. Find natural alternatives to chemical hair dyes.
- Work with a holistic doctor to develop a protocol of antioxidants, vitamins and herbal supplements to boost your immune system and reduce your risk of cancer (see Step 6).
- Don't live in fear of cancer. Having a strong mental attitude and dealing with your emotions are very important. Studies indicate that suppressing anger, fear, grief and sadness is linked to a higher incidence of cancer. And researchers working with women who had advanced breast cancer were surprised to find ten years later that the ones who'd been in support groups had survived twice as long as the women who'd had the same medical treatment but who weren't in support groups. These support groups had given the women an opportunity to express and share emotions about their cancer.
- Consider the big picture. A 1997 world conference on breast cancer in Kingston, Ontario, reported that ingesting an overload of chemicals and being exposed to environmental pollution significantly increase our risk of all cancers. This may well explain why so many cancer deaths aren't attributable to the previously identified risk factors. Toxic overload of our environment and our bodies may prove to be a major cause of cancer.

Dr. James Houston, a physician in Victoria who has been practising complementary, or holistic, medicine for many years, explains that "chemical toxins (additives, pesticides, preservatives), physical toxins (x-rays, electromagnetic fields from computers, electric blankets etc. and solar radiation), and emotional toxins (stress) bypass or overwhelm the body's detoxification systems such as those in the liver and gut."

According to Dr. Houston, when you eat bacon, ham or other cured meat, your body has to deal with the toxic nitrates. If your detoxification systems are strong they can handle these, but if they are already overburdened by toxins, this can create problems for the liver and gut and for the kidney, skin, bowels and the lungs—all involved in excreting toxins. For example, the majority of skin problems are related to an overload of toxins, but are seldom treated as such. Toxins are also a major cause of immune suppression.

Unfortunately, many dermatologists prescribe long-term antibiotics to keep the symptoms of skin problems in check. Not only does this approach not deal with the root cause, it can exacerbate the problem, and other symptoms will probably erupt. A dermatologist once told me that he had had patients on the drug tetracycline for ten years with no side effects. I wonder if those patients would have had something to add about other symptoms, but these people are probably going to other specialists for them. Not only is this segmented approach very costly to the health care system, but it's also costly to the patient's health. (This same doctor dismissed my query about toxins.)

Andrew Weil, M.D., a Harvard-educated medical pioneer, warns in his best seller *Spontaneous Healing* (Fawcett Columbine):

> Toxins can damage DNA, which contains the information needed for spontaneous healing; disrupt the biological controls on which the healing system depends; weaken defenses; and promote the development of cancer and other diseases.
>
> Toxic overload may be a significant cause of allergy, auto immune disease, and a variety of diseases like Parkinson's disease and ALS [amyotrophic lateral sclerosis]. The medical profession and the scientific research community have been remarkably slow to pay attention to this issue, which I consider to be one of the greatest threats to health and well-being in the world today.

One out of four people today will develop some form of cancer. We need to know why so many of us are getting cancer and how to reduce our risk.

Start by reducing the amount of toxins you eat and breathe. I don't feel hard-done-by not eating turkey sausage with nitrates or potato chips with the potentially carcinogenic preservatives BHA and BHT. (You can buy these products without these chemicals.) Once you know how to make healthier choices, it can be fairly simple. The key is to have awareness.

Marie's Risk Reduction Plan

To help her quit smoking, I encouraged Marie to get acupuncture from a highly qualified practitioner—not a beginner or even an M.D. who took a few weekend courses. She had tried acupuncture before and dismissed it as ineffective, but when she went to an experienced acupuncturist, she was able to quit smoking.

I also encouraged her to see a naturopathic physician, who prescribed a protocol of immune-boosting supplements. This plan significantly increased her energy and resistance to infections. Before, she would get recurring infections, go off to her regular doctor and get yet another course of antibiotics. Now, with a stronger immune system and an arsenal of natural and very effective ways to fight off the infection, she seldom resorts to antibiotics.

The naturopath tested her for allergies and found she was allergic to wheat, coffee, alcohol, sugar and nicotine, the very things she craved. Whenever she consumed those things, they would suppress her immune system and drag down her energy levels. When her immune system was stronger, Marie was able to gradually reintroduce all except nicotine, with no ill effects.

How Your Wondrous Immune System Works for You

Your immune system consists of billions and billions of little cells that keep your body as free as possible of harmful bacteria, germs, viruses and pollution. It's a complex and wonderful system that manages to keep most of us healthy most of the time despite the toxins that bombard us.

We know that cigarettes and many industrial and agricultural chemicals are toxic to our bodies (and to our environment). But there's a whole new area of research into the miraculous workings of our immune system. It's called "psychoneuroimmunology," also known as "mind/body medicine." Now, it may seem obvious that the mind and body are connected, but for the past hundred years, medical science has been trying to convince us otherwise.

Scientists have been finding out more and more about the physiological mechanisms that connect the brain and nervous system with the hormonal and immune systems. They're looking at how emotions affect health, and, in some instances, have confirmed that high levels of mismanaged stress damage the body's ability to fight disease.

Stress and the Immune System

In a series of experiments examining the effects of stress, medical students at Ohio State University had their white blood cell activity measured at mid-semester. Their cell activity was within the normal range. Then, just before exams, their blood was tested again. There was a significant decrease in B cells (which recognize invaders) and in T cells (which help destroy invaders). Since other factors remained constant and exams have been proven to be highly stressful, it was deduced that the stress response produced this decrease in white blood cell activity.

Here are some other interesting findings:

- Scientists have discovered that there is a two-way communication system between the mind and the immune system.
- Research has found that in individuals under stress, there was a marked decline in the production of the cells that kill virus-infected cells and other types of immune cells. It has also been shown that when people suffer a stressful trauma, such as the death of a child or spouse, there is a significant decrease in their white cell activity. This compromises the immune system's ability to fight off common complaints such as colds and flu, and the more dangerous diseases like cancer.
- Adrenalin and cortisol, two of the hormones produced when the body is under short-term or chronic stress, are also potent inhibitors of the immune system.

A strong immune system is an important component of keeping our fuel tank topped up. Dr. Weil advises, "If you want to increase the likelihood of spontaneous healing, it is imperative that you learn to guard against toxic injury. That means limiting exposure, protecting your body from the effects of pollution, and helping your body eliminate any toxins that do get in."

I highly recommend his books *Spontaneous Healing* and *Eight Weeks to Optimum Health* (Knopf), and his Web site (http://www.drweil.com).

Now that we have assessed our health account and the factors working for and against us, let's see how we can minimize our debits and maximize our credits. This strategy will boost our stamina and longevity. As healthy A's, we can live our lives fully, in the bloom of health, for many years to come.

STEP 6

Boost Your Health

Nature provides the human body and its immune system with an incredible array of anticancer, antibacterial, antiviral, antidisease supports called phytochemicals and antioxidants, which are found in many common foods—extremely potent sources I call Superfoods. These health-giving foods are toxic-waste collectors patrolling your body to protect your cells and bloodstream from the ever-growing chemical threats in our environment.

Sam Graci
The Power of Superfoods

A few winters ago, my husband and I were in the incredibly polluted capital cities of London, Delhi and Kathmandu. Six weeks gagging on exhaust fumes is enough to turn any mindless gas guzzler into an environmentalist. You see pretty quickly what it will be like when our streets are choked with vehicles and our air is choked with poisonous pollution. Clean air and clean water will become very precious commodities. We returned home with a nasty respiratory flu, and I developed asthma-like reactions to chemicals. A short time later, I had lunch with two dear friends, both well perfumed (and knowing them, it wasn't cheap stuff). I started to wheeze. I went home, got a large garbage bag and routed through the house, tossing out anything perfumed, scented or cologned and all chemical cleaning products. The bag was soon full. Into the recycling bin. (Now I buy fragrance-free, non-toxic cleaning supplies, soaps, shampoos, and I never wear perfume.)

Environmentalist David Steinman warns about the hazards of added fragrance in his book, *Living Healthy in a Toxic World* (Perigee): "Six hundred or more chemical ingredients may be used in a single scent and ninety-five percent of chemicals used in scents are derived from petroleum—many of which are designated as hazardous waste disposal chemicals."

Reducing our exposure to allergens and toxins will significantly boost our health. It's an on-going challenge that starts at home.

Cleaning Up a Toxic House

There seem to be a lot more people reporting allergies and asthma these days. Part of the reason may be the increasing number of pollutants in our air and pesticides and preservatives in our food.

The natural world has its share of allergens too, including dust, pollen, moulds and mildew. We are starting to hear more about people who are so sensitive to environmental and other toxins that they have to be extremely careful of what they eat, wear, sleep in, breathe, drink and clean with.

Their homes have to be built from non-toxic materials. They can't be around people wearing toxic chemical-based perfumes. Some of these people have lived with impaired health for years; some have found themselves almost completely debilitated.

It's only in the past decade or so that environmental illness has been recognized as a real syndrome, and that people who suffer from it have shed the label "hypochondriac."

Symptoms can include things like headaches, flulike symptoms, respiratory reactions, skin rashes, muscle weakness, joint pains, extreme fatigue and depression (though whether depression is part of the syndrome or the natural result of feeling lousy all the time is still being explored).

The "sick building syndrome" is also becoming recognized, as our poorly ventilated buildings leave us in a toxic soup of construction glues, paints, chemically treated carpets, pressed-wood furniture and so on. Some people who live or work in buildings like this complain they feel as though they're coming down with flu all the time; these symptoms miraculously disappear once these workers have been out in the fresh air for a half hour.

Fortunately, most of us don't have that level of extreme sensitivity, but our poor old overtaxed immune systems do have trouble dealing with all the extra stresses.

Here are a few tips for minimizing some of the environmental load on your immune system and on your family's:

- Vacuum frequently to get rid of dust and animal dander (especially if you have pets). Use those new micro-filter bags.
- Clean out your furnace filter often. (Did you know your furnace had a filter that needed cleaning?) You can also put a few layers of cheesecloth over the air grates to catch the dust or get filters made for that purpose.
- Choose hard surfaces like wood floors and ceramic tile when it's time to renovate or build a new house; these surfaces are easier to keep clean than carpets. Or you can use small throw rugs that can be washed. New carpets and linoleum give off toxic fumes for some time.
- Make sure your basement is well ventilated to discourage the growth of moulds and mildew.
- Use more environmentally friendly cleaning products, such as white vinegar, baking soda, borax and some of the new natural cleaning agents. I get all my cleaning supplies at the natural foods store. They work just as well and are non-toxic. Regular commercial products are usually loaded with harsh additives. (I hope you are not still using chemical-laden room deodorizer in your home or your car. I avoid a local post office outlet located in a gift shop because of the fumes from all the lovely looking packets of pot-pourri and sachets that are drenched with toxic fragrances.)
- Whenever possible, use non-toxic or less toxic home improvement products; there are now low-odour, water-based paints, varnishes and glues.
- Open the windows and let the fresh air in (at least, that's good advice in places like Victoria, with its clean air, but if you're in a polluted, industrial area, you may be better off with closed windows and an air purifier).
- Don't nuke your garden with poisonous sprays. There are less toxic or even completely natural ways to deal with pests and weeds. And more natural gardens, using indigenous, disease-resistant plants, are becoming popular.

It may take a little research into what's available in your city or town, and some time to get into a new pattern of where you shop and what you buy. But finding more health-giving ways to feed your family and clean your house can be an enjoyable challenge. Better for all of you and for this good earth.

We've looked at how to reduce some of the debit demands on our immune system and overall health account. Now let's look at some great ways to credit that account and refuel and recharge.

Boosting Your Immune System

Green Superfoods

Foods that boost immunity are the most valuable investments in our port-folio. If you're tired a lot of the time, your immune system is probably weak-ened. One avenue that more and more people are investigating is that of so-called superfoods: spirulina and other algae, seaweed, wheat grass, bar-ley grass, sprouts, alfalfa, chlorella and chlorophyll. These immune-boosting green foods from land and sea are good detoxifiers, blood cleansers and sources of minerals, enzymes and other nutrients.

Some "smart bars" and vegetarian restaurants whip these superfoods up in their blenders; you can do the same at home, mixing them with apple or carrot juice and fresh ginger. It's a great way to perk up when you are feel-ing burnt out or coming down with a cold.

These power drinks provide high-octane fuel and are a big part of the Healthy Type A Program. I take my green drink every morning—for a dollar a day—less than a cappuccino, and much better fuel. You will find all the information you need to recharge your batteries and keep your energy up —without caffeine or sugar—in *The Power of Superfoods* by Sam Graci (Prentice-Hall). Making a superfood power drink part of your day is one of the best things you can do for your health and stamina.

Of all the green foods, one that seems to hold great promise is blue-green algae. Many health practitioners recommend this algae to treat a wide range of illnesses, particularly immune suppression. Algae is also reported to have a beneficial effect on organs, the brain and the nervous system. Algae pro-vides the nutrients to rebuild our cells and enhances the detoxification process—both essential elements in maintaining good health.

Antioxidants

Vitamins C, E, A, beta-carotene, zinc, selenium, coenzyme Q10 and grape seed extract protect the body from molecules called "free radicals," which are now believed to be quite harmful to our health. They can form when we're exposed to toxic chemicals, too much sun and second-hand smoke. Free radicals damage cells and hurt the immune system; this damage can eventually lead to infections, heart disease and cancer. The most powerful antioxidant may by coenzyme Q10, which is being studied intensely all over the world, especially for its dramatic benefits for people with heart disease. Medical pioneers tuned into the specific challenges of our increasingly polluted cities are strong proponents of use of these supplements. I asked Dr. Dean how she dealt with the pollution of New York City, and she replied, "For one, I take a lot of antioxidants."

Natural Vitamin Supplements

Natural vitamins are worth the investment. Dr. Michael Colgan, a noted biochemist and author of several books on nutrition, recommends the USANA vitamin program, which contains high-quality, balanced vitamins, minerals and antioxidants.

Ginseng

The Chinese have sworn by this vitality-producing root for thousands of years. It enhances immune function, makes several glands function better, gives energy and stimulates the nervous system. It may also lower blood cholesterol. Some varieties are better for women and some for men, so it's best to do some research before treating yourself. (Dr. Dean advises most women not to use ginseng until the menopausal years.)

Bee Pollen

This is produced by plants and gathered by bees. It is helpful for managing allergy symptoms as well as boosting the immune system. It's best to use locally produced pollen.

Bee Propolis

This is also from plants by way of the bees. And it is also useful in fighting bacterial infections and is thought to stimulate the growth of white blood cells, which fight off infection.

Royal Jelly

This substance comes from bees and, as well as stimulating the immune system, is used for bronchial asthma and skin disorders.

A Confident Attitude

Seeing yourself as being in control—rather than as a victim in a situation—enhances the strength of your immune system.

New Roads to Wellness

Dr. Balch is in the vanguard of the new medicine. During his career, he drifted away from the style of medicine that relies mostly on pills and surgery and has embraced a more holistic view.

Most health practitioners occupy one of two opposing camps: on one side, we have the pharmaceutical-based approach, which relies heavily on drugs, lab tests and surgery. These tools can save lives, and we wouldn't want to be without them. Problems arise, however, if they're the only options, or if they're overused.

On the other side, we have the natural "alternative" therapies, such as acupuncture, homeopathy and nutritional healing, which rely on supplements, herbs, vitamins and techniques designed to strengthen the body's inner resources. Problems can arise if the practitioner is not fully trained and qualified.

In the middle ground is complementary or integrated medicine. This approach brings together the best of both approaches and considers the whole person and the whole picture. A range of treatment options are considered; antibiotics may be prescribed, but usually not as the first line of defence. This emerging blend of approaches can be confusing.

If your doctor is not up-to-date with the current alternatives to prescription drugs and surgery, you might suggest he or she review this book. If your doctor regards this suggestion as out-of-hand and usually dismisses your questions, you might consider finding a doctor who keeps listening and learning and is up-to-date.

Patients and practitioners alike benefit from the guidance of experts like Dr. James Balch. He graduated with honours from Indiana University's School of Medicine and has been a successful specialist and surgeon for many years. With Phyllis Balch, he wrote the ground-breaking book *Prescription for Nutritional Healing* (Avery), and shared some of his wisdom in an interview I did with him in Victoria, British Columbia.

K.C.: What is nutritional healing?
Dr. Balch: It's the use of nutritionally based, drug-free remedies and therapies that are effective and much safer than drugs. These include the proper use of vitamins, minerals, herbs and food supplements.

K.C.: Can you explain the benefits of vitamin C and E and other antioxidants?
Dr. Balch: Antioxidants are a group of vitamins and minerals, also including vitamin A and selenium, which act as scavengers to neutralize atoms called free radicals. Free radicals can damage our cells, impair our immune system and lead to infections and degenerative diseases such as cancer.

K.C.: Why should we take vitamins if we're eating well?

Dr. Balch: Our food is grown on soil with fewer nutrients and has been more processed than ever before. And we're being bombarded with more stress, toxins and pollutants.

K.C.: Why take larger doses than the recommended daily allowance?

Dr. Balch: The RDA was established more than 40 years ago—the environment, and our needs, have changed considerably. We need much higher levels than the out-dated RDA. Sixty milligrams for vitamin C, for example, is far too low—a single cigarette can take out that amount. Higher levels are safe. Dr. Abram Hoffer, another Victoria physician . . . points out that the RDA were established to set the minimum amount that would prevent you from getting a deficiency disease—the amount of vitamin C to prevent scurvy, for example.

K.C.: Why do you recommend natural vitamins when some cost more?

Dr. Balch: Our body absorbs natural vitamins much better. And they are better balanced—ascorbic acid is vitamin C, but it's missing bioflavinoids, an important element. And natural vitamins don't cost much more. They are worth the bit extra.

K.C.: What about taking antacids for calcium?

Dr. Balch: This is a very poor way to get calcium and not a good way to deal with hyperacidity. And recent studies say aluminum in antacid tablets, if taken long enough, may soften and weaken your bones.

K.C.: Are digestive enzymes helpful?

Dr. Balch: Yes. Because we lack live enzymes. Most of our food is cooked and processed. Best to get the kind that don't contain hydrochloric acid. Enzymes should be taken just before eating.

K.C.: How do your medical colleagues view your approach?

Dr. Balch: Many doctors send their families and friends to see me. And they "admit" to using our book *Prescription for Nutritional Healing* under the table as a reference guide.

K.C.: Why don't most doctors tell us about these things?

Dr. Balch: Doctors are trained to think of a pill for every ill. If the pills don't work then we send patients to the surgeon. And we order too many expensive, and unnecessary, tests.

K.C.: And we wonder why our health care costs are soaring out of control. If you were minister of health, what would you do first?

Dr. Balch: Health care administrators don't seem to get the picture—if budgets are a problem you want to practice preventive medicine. Prevention is the key. I would heed what the public is demanding. And we need to teach doctors in pre-medicine to understand what the body requires to stay healthy. We need to update these doctors' knowledge about the benefits of natural remedies and how and when to use them.

K.C.: What if my doctor doesn't believe in this approach?

Dr. Balch: If yours doesn't, ask around. You have to be a searcher and a seeker.

The following are Dr. Balch's recommendations to boost your health.

1. *Cut back on animal products, including dairy.* Red meat—for men—can be a killer; we know it's linked to prostate cancer. For women, red meat may turn out to be a factor in breast cancer. Chicken is better, but not much, because of how it's handled. Fish is the best choice. I love meat but I've learned that it's not good for me, so I've cut down on it. Eat more whole foods like vegetables, grains and fruits. Raw foods have lots of enzymes and are very good for us.

2. *Drink good-quality water.* Water is key to our good health— we're 75 percent water. As we age we don't drink enough. Be sure to drink a 6-ounce. glass of water, not coffee or tea, every few hours that you're awake. If possible, drink water from a good filtration system and avoid tap water. Clean, good-quality water is a worthwhile investment. Do some research.

3. *Take natural supplements.* In this high stress world, you need to supplement your diet with Vitamin C, a quality multi-vitamin, Kyolic garlic (a deodorized brand) and a good antioxidant formula like grape seed extract. The green formulas—like Kyogreen —are also beneficial.

K.C.: What do you recommend for arthritis?

Dr. Balch: Kyolic garlic, evening primrose oil, alfalfa, and the antioxidants. Lots of good quality water. Potatoes, tomatoes, peppers and dairy are not helpful.

K.C.: What is your view of hormonal replacement therapy?

Dr. Balch: I am very against this—artificial estrogens are carcinogenic—evidence is overwhelming that they're related to breast cancer, uterine cancer, cervical cancer. There are many safe natural estrogens—dong quai, vitamin E, evening primrose oil. Wild yam, also a herb, acts like progesterone.

I also asked Dr. Dean about hormone replacement. She concurs with Dr. Balch and cautions against synthetic hormone replacement therapy and recommends natural alternatives—progestin cream and tri-estrogen supplements. These are available from more progressive pharmacies.

Sam Graci also encourages us to drink more filtered, or bottled, water. "Water is needed for all the chemical reactions in the body. Without enough water, optimum efficiency levels fall. When the water supply is short, the body starts rationing it—taking water away from the skin, hair, mouth, and throat, and giving it to the essential organs. We get more colds because our sinuses are dry, and our skin ages more quickly."

I carry a bottle of filtered water most places I go and drink it throughout the day. And I keep a water bottle at my desk. These may seem like small things, but they are giving your body more of what it really needs. Minimizing debits and maximizing credits is how we boost our health account.

Please be aware that when your health account is chronically low, you have few reserves when a crisis hits. A loved one is dying, a loved one leaves you, a child gets sick, you get sick, the business goes under, you get laid off. During a crisis we seldom have any energy for embarking on new health-giving activities. It is so important to build up our health while we've still got it.

Putting These Strategies into Action

Making positive changes in our lifestyle isn't easy, but healthy Type A's know the short- and long-term benefits of taking better care of ourselves sooner. We're motivated and we've woken up from the slumber of ignorance.

Here are a few tips for putting all these suggestions into action:

- *Be realistic.* The biggest myth is that "it won't happen to me."
- *Be informed.* If you've read this far, you're more informed than most.
- *Be kind to yourself.* It takes a while to break old habits. Expect set-backs and don't be discouraged; they are part of the process. Keep going.
- *Be proactive.* If you have a heart attack or your biopsy test indicates

cancer, you will make the time to get in shape or find the motivation to quit smoking. Doesn't it make more sense to make those changes now?

- *Be in charge.* As you may have noticed, the fitness patrol is not going to drag you from your desk or off the couch, snatch those fries from your hand and get you out for some exercise. Take charge and start your own exercise plan.

Your live-it-up buddies are right: we're not going to live forever. But let's appreciate this precious human body and all it does. Let's realize that feeling healthy is not a gift. It is something we earn. And the times are changing to make this proactive approach more accessible, and there is a wealth of resources to guide us in this new direction.

Boosting your health includes taking stock of your risks, which you did in the last step, and taking charge of your health by seeing how your symptoms may be connected and seeking out the cause, and by boosting your health with superfoods and supplements. Another vital step is to build a team of complementary practitioners. On my team, I have a holistic physician, an acupuncturist, a naturopath, a chiropractor and a massage therapist. I don't see them all that often, but this kind of support and expertise is an important component of being a healthy Type A.

7-7   © 1976 Jim Unger

"Are you eating properly and getting plenty of exercise?"

Your Health Team

You've probably been hearing or reading about some of the "new" therapies (some of which are thousands of years old), but may not know much about them. I've asked some of my colleagues, here in Victoria, to describe their disciplines.

Holistic Medicine

James Tucker, M.D., is a physician who has been practising medicine for nearly 30 years, most of that time in a holistic way. Dr. Tucker describes this approach:

> It combines traditional western medicine which deals mostly with symptoms and energy medicine which deals mostly with intangibles, such as *chi* (pronounced chee—this is the life force energy found in every human being and in the world around us).
>
> It's good to start out from the Western approach, as that is known territory, and then to reach out to energy medicine which includes homeopathy, herbs, Chinese medicine, acupuncture and most body therapies. The focus here is on the interconnectedness of the body and mind, also called "mind/body" medicine. The next realm is to approach healing the human condition, or the pain and suffering all around us. Most people I see today are sick at what I call a spirit level—they are worn down, their chi, or life force is low. This is often related to the excessive speed of our culture, childhood shock and trauma, and a sense of disconnectedness—not being connected to each other, to themselves, or nature. I believe there's a transformational possibility based on a fundamental healthiness in the mind/body which we may have lost or covered up, but which is still there. In my work, I try to assist the person in boosting their *chi* energy, in reconnecting, and in rediscovering their basic healthiness.

Naturopathy

Lisa Connoly, N.D., is a naturopathic physician who has integrated naturopathic and TCM in her practice for 14 years. Dr. Connoly says,

> Naturopathic Medicine encompasses many health sciences and philosophies and holds and reflects, in its practice, the following principles:

The Healing Power of Nature. Recognizing that each organism has the ability to heal itself given the proper environment.

Identify and Treat the Cause. When the body's natural balance is disrupted, the body communicates its imbalance by symptoms of distress. These signs and symptoms are often grouped together and labelled a disease process. While being aware of the "disease" or symptomology it is important to look beyond these to determine the true cause.

Doctor as Teacher. Sharing our knowledge with our patients, and with others, gives each person the ability to be responsible for their own health and helps them make informed decisions.

First Do No Harm. It is important, in diagnosis or in treatment, to use the least invasive methods possible.

Treat the Whole Person. Health is a complex interaction of physical, mental, emotional, genetic, environmental, social, and spiritual factors.

As a Naturopathic physician I respect each of these principles when looking at a person's health. This results in an individualized and comprehensive approach to diagnosis and treatment. Some of the tools used in naturopathic practice are:

- Clinical and laboratory testing
- Nutrition and food sciences
- Botanical medicine—the use of plants to stimulate healing
- Homeopathy—diluted amounts of plants or minerals to stimulate healing
- Psychotherapy and counselling
- Traditional Chinese medicine—the use of herbs and acupuncture
- Physical medicine—the use of heat, cold, water, massage, exercise and electrotherapy

Acupuncture and Traditional Chinese Medicine

If you haven't had acupuncture because you don't like needles, let me allay your fears. Acupuncture needles are very fine; this treatment is not like having blood taken or an injection. You feel sensation when the needle is on a point where energy is blocked. I relate to this positively as I know energy is being released and reduces pain and heals symptoms.

Dr. Hong Zhu is the chief instructor of the Canadian College of Acupuncture in Victoria. He has been teaching and practising acupuncture for more than 20 years.

Acupuncture has been used for more than 5,000 years as a preventative and curative system of healing. It is based on the system of pathways, or meridians, through which vital *chi* energy flows through the body. The meridians run just beneath the surface of the skin and also connect with the internal organs. By inserting thin, solid needles into specific points along the meridians, it is possible to disperse the blockages of *chi* and correct various organ imbalances by draining excess energy where too much has accumulated, or by stimulating more *chi* where there is not enough.

The aim of the acupuncturist is to correct the flow of *chi* and thereby affect a change in the body. Changes in *chi* precede physical, and even mental and emotional change. So acupuncture can act as preventative medicine, correcting the energy before a serious illness can occur. Also, acupuncture treats the root of the imbalance, not just the symptoms, by adjusting the flow of *chi*.

Acupuncture works by restoring an energetic balance to the body to re-establish its rhythm with the natural cycles of the seasons, day and night, and the time of day. As the *chi* blockages and imbalances are corrected, the person's body, mind and spirit start to heal.

While acupuncture is most commonly known in North America for the treatment of pain, and drug detoxification, the World Health Organization now recognizes the ability of acupuncture to treat many common clinical disorders.

How to find a good acupuncturist:

Make sure to ask these three basic questions:
1. Where did you do your training, and for how many years? (We recommend the training be at least 3 years long at an established school.)
2. How many years have you been practising?
3. Do you use disposable single use needles? (This is recommended.)

I go to see Dr. Zhu for acupuncture when I need to ward off a cold, boost my energy or heal a strained muscle. In my experience, you need to find a very experienced practitioner. Acupuncture works on a different system than

These conditions may respond to acupuncture:

Addictions
Allergies
Arthritis
Asthma
Acne
Back pain
Circulation problems
Chronic fatigue syndrome/fibromyalgia
Colds/flu/bronchitis
Depression/anxiety
Gastro-intestinal disorders
Heart problems/high blood pressure
Headaches
Herpes
Immune deficiencies
Infertility
Insomnia
Joint pain/stiffness
Menstrual problems/PMS/menopausal symptoms
Sexual dysfunction
Skin problems
Sports Injuries
Stress
Weight gain or loss

Western medicine. To be effective, the fine needles need to be right on the point, and the targets are tiny. I knew a physician who got a diagram and some needles and started firing them into people. Eventually, he gave it up because, he said, "this acupuncture only works as a placebo. I didn't find it very effective at all." I tried to explain about it being a different system, about *chi* and the meridian pathways and about taking pulses. He gave me a blank stare.

Acupuncture and Allergies

My brother Barry Crofton, who trained with Dr. Zhu, is an acupuncturist practising in Wolfville, Nova Scotia, and Halifax. He specializes in the treatment of environmental illness and allergies using the Nambudripad Allergy Elimination Technique (NAET). He describes this method:

> NAET combines kinesiology—how structural balance and the central nervous system affect movement and energy flow—chiro-

practic and acupuncture knowledge to affect the relaxation of the nervous system in response to an allergen. This treatment strengthens the immune system and can result in the direct cessation of an allergic response. For instance, people who have been anaphylactic or seriously allergic to chocolate or peanuts can now eat them without incident and those who have been house bound by environmental sensitivities are once again leading normal productive lives.

Those interested in reaching health professionals who practice this method may contact the Dr. Devi S. Nambudripad Pain Clinic, 6714 Beach Blvd., Buena Park, CA, 90621, tel. 714-523-0800 for a list of certified practitioners.

Homeopathy

Stephen Malthouse, M.D., has been a physician in general practice for nearly 20 years. Several years ago he began to specialize in homeopathic medicine. He describes this classical healing tradition:

Homeopathy is a unique system of medicine based upon natural laws of healing. It provides safe, effective treatment for mental, emotional and physical ailments. Homeopathic medicines act by stimulating the body's own recuperative powers, or vital force allowing the body to heal itself and return to a state of optimum health. Treatment is aimed at removing the cause of illness rather than trying to eliminate the symptoms alone. Homeopathy recognizes that each individual will experience symptoms of disease in a unique way and endeavours to match the total disease picture to a single medicine.

The Origin of Homeopathy

Homeopathy was formulated by the German physician Samuel Hahnemann almost 200 years ago. However, the natural law upon which homeopathy is based was known to physicians dating back many centuries.

How Does It Work?

The Law of Similars states that a medicinal substance, which can cause certain symptoms when taken by a healthy person, can cure those same symptoms when given to a sick patient. Examples can be found in conventional medicine. Nitroglycerin, if taken in large quantities, can cause rapid heart rate, shortness of breath and chest pain—the same symptoms that a small medicinal dose of nitro-glycerin under the tongue can relieve. In everyday life, exposure to onion juice leads to burning and watery eyes, runny nose and sneezing. Prepared homeopathically, onion (allium cepa) is one of the many effective remedies for hayfever.

What Illnesses Can Homeopathy Treat?

Homeopathy is used for the treatment of both acute and chronic health problems. Minor ailments of short duration, such as colds, flu, digestive upsets or injuries, can be resolved quickly. More deep-seated illnesses, such as eczema, allergies, arthritis or depression, require a longer course of treatment with a remedy for your overall health.

Chiropractic

Sheel Tangri, D.C., is an innovative chiropractor with 11 years' experience. His approach includes conventional chiropractic adjustments to balance the spine, but he also incorporates kinesiology and other holistic techniques to reset the central nervous system, and he focuses on the emotional and spiritual aspects of healing. Dr. Tangri says,

> Chiropractic is a science and an art based on the philosophy that the nervous system is one of the primary vehicles of energy flow in the body. Much like an intricate computer, the nervous system regulates the function of almost every cell in the body. Therefore, if there is interference in this flow of energy, the person cannot maintain an optimum level of balance and survival in an increasingly stressful environment. The person now descends out of optimum health and begins the journey through varying states of disease and "un-wellness."

The Focus of Chiropractic

Dr. Tangri describes his field:

> Chiropractic focuses on restoring the flow of energy in the nervous system. There are three main causes of nervous system interference:

1. *Physical:* Birth traumas, falls, car and bike accidents, and sports injuries create mechanical misalignments and fixations of the frame, particularly the spine and cranium, which protect the delicate nervous system.
2. *Emotional:* Stressful events such as job and family stress, death and loss drain the energy flow which usually will manifest as a physical symptom, unless one is taking adequate time to meditate, exercise or find a constructive way of releasing old or new stress patterns,
3. *Chemical:* Foods, additives, pollution, and detergents shock the body from the inside, creating poor energy flow.

There is a broad spectrum of techniques being developed and performed by different chiropractors all around the world. One involves aligning the spinal vertebrae; another is called "neural organization technique," which resets the central nervous system through subtle physical adjustments. All are based, however, on the principles listed above.

One must find the Doctor of Chiropractic who is best suited to individual needs. It's important to remember that many health problems begin very early in life, well before the symptoms appear, so a proactive approach is helpful.

Massage Therapy

Glenn Timms, R.M.T. (Registered Massage Therapist), has had a professional practice for 16 years and sees many people with low back, neck and head pain.

In these cases, I massage the muscles and loosen restrictions in joints in the problem area, and associated areas. My intent is to neutralize trigger points—very tender places in the muscles that perpetuate many musculoskeletal syndromes such as low back pain and tension headache. I also use a variety of techniques to balance energy flow— the chi—and restore the natural rhythm of the craniosacral system— the plates that form the skull. To find a good practitioner, contact the regional massage therapy association and ask about qualified practitioners in your area.

Biofeedback

Thomas Budzynski, Ph.D., is one of the pioneers in this field and has been on the leading edge of research for 30 years. Dr. Budzynski explains,

> Biofeedback involves the "feeding back" of biological responses related to a specific problem, or disorder. The client, hooked up to monitors, sees a meter, or hears a series of beeps, reflecting skin temperature, muscle tension, heart rate or brainwaves. This allows the client to gain control over these aspects of his or her physiology.
>
> For example, stress is a factor in your muscle pain. Sensors placed on your skin measure the muscle tension and you receive precise, moment-to-moment feedback. This information, enhanced by relaxation techniques, helps you reduce this tension—and the pain. You also learn to recognize the subtle clues that you're tensing this muscle so you can do your stretching and breathing *before* it goes into a painful spasm. Another benefit—this training procedure significantly reduces, or eliminates, the need for over-the-counter, or prescription, drugs.
>
> Biofeedback is effective in the treatment of a wide variety of disorders such as high blood pressure, headache, insomnia, chronic pain, Attention Deficit Disorder, stroke, muscle rehabilitation, addictions, panic attacks, stress and PTSD (Post Traumatic Stress Disorder). New areas of research include peak performance, cognitive enhancement in the elderly, PMS, and Chronic Fatigue Syndrome.

I trained as a biofeedback therapist with Dr. Budzynski years ago. Even two decades later, biofeedback is underutilized. This is unfortunate, as it's a potent tool for harnessing the power of the mind. Researchers have trained laboratory rats to control blood flow and raise the temperature in one ear and lower it in the other, simultaneously. Imagine what we can do.

Counselling

Emotional well-being is a large part of being a healthy Type A, so a skilled counsellor can be a vital member of your team. Having a supportive, yet impartial, listener can help you ventilate and sort out your feelings. He or she can also provide insight into your habitual patterns and inspire you to take charge; feeling helpless to change the course of our lives is at the root of many difficulties, such as depression.

I believe that we need to take a close look at our patterns and our motivations, and to sift through our past. I don't, however, feel we should get stuck there. All of us have suffered pain and protect places where we feel wounded. It is helpful to uncover these events, perhaps even re-experience them, but then we need to let them go. It is not helpful to hold on to negative beliefs about ourselves, our parents or anyone else. The challenge is to let things arise, to see them without judgement and to let them go.

When to Seek Counselling

As a counsellor, I was often saddened when working with a couple or family blocked by what I call the "too much water under the bridge" syndrome—too many angry things said and done, too much hurt, too much distrust. These obstacles can become insurmountable. Therefore, I strongly encourage you to seek counselling *before* the situation reaches that point.

Take charge when your communication feels too hot—when your anger flares up too quickly and you say or do things that you later regret—or when it's too cold—you feel distant and closed off from others. An inner voice may scoff, "You don't need a professional. It is a sign of weakness to . . ." However, seeking the assistance of a skilled counsellor is a sign of strength and bravery.

How to Find a Good Counsellor

Before you go searching for a counsellor, consider the types of professionals available: psychiatrists are M.D.'s and can prescribe medications, psychologists may have been trained in experimental or clinical/counselling psychology, and counsellors may have a B.A. or M.A. in psychology or counselling. But it's not only the training that matters; the human qualities are important too. It's best to look for both.

Use your own intuition. Avoid these two extremes: a person who has the credentials but seems cold, critical and distant, or an overbearing helper who has to fix everything up quickly so you—and he or she—will be okay. A skilled practitioner will be encouraging, will enlighten you and will inspire you to move forward. Rather than boosting their own ego with their great advice, good counsellors are more interested in your learning from situations and discovering your innate confidence and clarity.

How to Find a Good Health Care Practitioner

Here are some guidelines provided by Dr. Stephen Malthouse.

1. Educate yourself about your health problems. Go to the library or a bookstore and try searching the Internet. Contact local self-help groups.

2. Research the therapies that interest you and learn about the benefits and the risks.

3. Try to find a practitioner who has a holistic approach. Holism (from the Greek word *holos*, meaning "entire") is an understanding of how the body and mind are interconnected and influence each other. Gather information about a local health care practitioner before making an appointment. Pay attention to training, credentials, reputation, experience and cost of services. A health care provider who is a member of an official association, college or training institution will provide a standard level of competency. But finding a practitioner through these organizations may not guarantee the best care. Although they are usually the exception to the rule, some practitioners with excellent healing skills have never registered in any training program.

When considering a practitioner, answer these questions:

- Do your family, friends, local support group, physician or other health care professional have any recommendations?
- How did the health care provider train in this particular therapy?
- How long has the practitioner been in practice?
- What are the fees? Are treatment costs covered by provincial or private health insurance?
- Aside from the consultation fee, are there any additional costs for supplements, medications or diagnostic tests?

Arrange an initial brief interview. Often there is no charge for this service. And it provides an opportunity for you and the practitioner to ask questions and assess the probability of successful treatment. Ask if the practitioner has treated people with your condition. What was the success rate? How long did treatment take? What is the prognosis in your case? Then ask yourself: Did I feel comfortable during the interview? Did I feel respected? Does the proposed treatment plan make sense to me?

I suggest you stick with your chosen therapy for enough time to give it a fair chance, keeping in mind that treatment results are directly related to the depth, duration and complexity of your illness. For most chronic conditions, you should see significant improvement within three to six months.

When choosing a practitioner, beware of these scenarios:
- The practitioner insists that you stop all other medications, and you are concerned about this request. In most cases, you can continue with conventional medications and discontinue them when your condition improves.
- Your conventional physician is not willing to cooperate with your plan for complementary treatment. Consider finding a more sympathetic and open-minded physician.
- The health care provider refuses to explain your treatment. A condescending or secretive attitude is both disrespectful and unproductive. Find a new practitioner.
- The health care provider thinks his or her method is the only way to treat your condition.
- You are having a prolonged healing crisis: your symptoms seem to be getting worse. Although some conditions may temporarily worsen with the start of complementary therapies, a prolonged worsening may be the result of side effects or inappropriate treatment.

In some cases where improvement is not seen, the lack of skill or experience of the practitioner, not the therapy itself, may be the cause of the failure. Do some more research and try to find another practitioner with more experience.

Natural Health Strategies

Here are some of the tips I've gathered over the years to help you take care of yourself when you need to:

Fight Off a Cold
When I feel a cold or flu coming on, I cut back on my activities as much as I can, keep warm and drink lots of hot liquids—but not coffee or rum! And I rely on a powerful herbal combination: echinacea, vitamin C, Kyolic garlic, goldenseal and zinc lozenges. All of these are available at the health food store or a progressive pharmacy.

Reduce Gastro-intestinal Problems
Hurrying and worrying can create havoc with digestion. Remember, digesting food is part of the rest mode. You don't have to go into a meditative trance every time you put something in your mouth, but it's helpful to breathe and relax when you eat. And please do not harangue your family at the dinner table.

Also try to forgo ice water, or any iced drinks with your meals, as the coldness inhibits the secretion of digestive enzymes and impairs your digestion. In addition, consider taking plant extract enzymes with meals.

Your doctor may have recommended antacids for your indigestion and as a cheap source of calcium. However, they contain aluminum and are not that good for your digestive system! And they are not a cure; seek the source of the symptoms and deal with it. For temporary relief, peppermint or ginger tea will settle the digestion and ease stomach upset. Acupuncture is also very helpful.

Help for Migraines

Some people, usually those with a family history of migraines, respond to stress primarily with a constriction of the blood vessels. These vessels can also overreact to various foods like cheese or beverages like red wine, which contains tyramine; nitrates in hot dogs and bacon; changes in the weather; and, for women, changes in their hormones. MSG, or monosodium glutamate, can be another culprit.

Some of these factors make the vessels constrict too much. As a result, the brain needs more oxygen, so it signals the vessels to dilate. But, in some people, the blood vessels dilate too much, causing pressure on the nerves and producing tremendous pain.

You saw in Step 2 that many migraine medications contain caffeine because it constricts the arteries, but it's a temporary solution at best. (If you suffer from migraines, you might consider coming off all caffeine very gradually.)

The problem is not that your blood vessels are too big, although that's causing the throbbing pain right now; the problem is that your blood vessels are too reactive. So you want to stay away from anything that makes them constrict *or* expand. This includes sugar and alcohol.

Some research suggests chronic migraine sufferers are perfectionists who are very hard on themselves. Please don't be hard on yourself about this. As you've read here, all of us need to ease up on the inner battle between our must-be-in-control side and our let-things-flow side. Easing up on ourselves eases our stress, which may be a factor in migraines. The relaxation techniques in Step 4 should be very helpful, particularly the hand warming technique. (Hand warming is even more effective when combined with biofeedback training.) Moreover, a good complementary care doctor will check for allergies, which are often the cause of migraine. He or she may suggest feverfew, a herb that has shown great promise in the prevention and treatment of migraine.

Ease the Pain of Tension Headaches

Some people's vulnerable spots are in their muscles. Muscles like to expand *and* contract, not just contract more and more throughout the day, causing fatigue, pain and spasm. Tension headaches are caused by tight muscles squeezing nerves and blood vessels. If you get them after hours of being hunched over a computer, try taking brief breaks more often.

Many people find doing the progressive relaxation exercises in Step 4—tensing up each individual body part, then letting go—very helpful. Your cue is probably a muscular one—please listen to it earlier. You also might consider finding a professional massage therapist to be part of your health team, as described earlier in this chapter.

Get Your Back in Shape

Back pain has been a problem for many of us since our ancestors decided to walk on their hind legs. If you have a bad back, how strong are your tummy muscles? Most bad backs can be improved or even cured by toning the abdominal muscles, which support the spine and pelvis.

Massage therapist Glenn Timms explains,

> Muscles are organs of movement. When a muscle is not utilized sufficiently it will either lose tone and become flabby or become tight and shortened. Both conditions result in a loss of strength, flexibility, endurance and circulation. Depending on the muscles involved, this can lead to a variety of body pain syndromes such as low back pain. This is because the balance of muscular support for the low back is thrown off, in part, by underutilized muscle groups. Regular activity, stretching and strengthening exercises are excellent for maintaining good functional activity in the musculoskeletal system.

Another source of back pain might be your desk chair. Too many hours at a stretch—or without a stretch!—tenses those muscles. Remember they also want to expand. Ergonomically designed work stations can be well worth the investment. Lumbar support in your chair is good; even a small pillow helps. A foot rest can take some of the strain off the lower back. And remember to take stretching and breathing breaks. Get some oxygen into those muscles—to say nothing of your brain. Stretching exercises (like yoga, t'ai chi, swimming or anything else that gently improves your flexibility) and progressive relaxation techniques are helpful.

Keep Your Eyes Healthy

Uninterrupted hours at the computer are *very* hard on your eyes. Please take frequent breaks. Look off into the distance to change your focus. Cover your eyes with the palms of your hands and rest your elbows on your desk for a few minutes and breathe. Also check with your optometrist about new protective coating for glasses to reduce computer-related eye strain. It isn't just that the font in the phone book and on business cards is getting smaller— our eyes are getting older. We need to take better care of them.

If you are a heavy smoker, you should know that the *New England Journal of Medicine* reports that people who smoke a pack or more a day double their chances of developing macular degeneration, an untreatable form of blindness. This disease is thought to occur because of the harmful chemicals in cigarettes and the reduction of blood and oxygen to the eye.

Also, please protect your eyes with good sunglasses. Dark lenses don't ensure good UV protection; check the label.

Take Care of Your Teeth

There's controversial new research on mercury amalgam fillings. One group of dentists vows to never use them again. Another group swears they're perfectly safe. The government dithers. (My dentist, Dr. David Philip, remarked, "Mercury is very toxic and must be handled with extreme care. How can your patient's mouth be the only safe place to put it?")

I've given you a lot to think about. But putting this information to use does not have to be a huge, time-consuming burden. Armed with this knowledge and sources of help when you need them, you can make wiser choices, in your daily life to boost your health. It does not have to be a depressing burden: It can be an enjoyable challenge.

I have been working with all of these strategies for many years, in my own life, and in my professional practice. I have learned that attitude is as important as action. It's not helpful to fearfully gulp down vitamins and be so anxious and stressed out about what you should and should not be eating. It's much better to remember to breathe properly and gear down into the rest mode at all times. When eating enjoy your food, sip one glass of wine, savour your healthful meal and laugh with your loved ones—truly enjoy the moment.

The Missing Diagnosis?

One of the best ways to boost your health is to boost your immune system. And one of the best ways to do that is to become more aware of what has been called "the missing diagnosis."

When I had a clinical practice, I saw many people like Mrs. J. Her physician's referral stated: "Mrs. J. is a severely depressed individual with passive/aggressive tendencies. She has migraine headaches . . . suspect she is trying to avoid having sex with her husband. She's difficult to treat . . ."

Not a very kind, nor a very accurate, assessment.

Mrs. J. comes to see me. I greet her warmly. "Mrs. J., I understand you have been through a lot. Please tell me a little about your life."

She recounts the pressures crowding in on her: caring for an aging parent, having difficulty with her teenaged children, dealing with a stressful job. I ask her about her health and am struck by the emerging theme of her symptoms.

"I had a lot of colds and flu last winter. I'm tired all the time and get a lot of headaches." It's easy to attribute these to stress, but is there something else going on?

I ask her to give me a brief history of her health. "I often had strep throat when I was a child; the doctors gave me lots of antibiotics. As a teen, I had problems with my menstrual cycle; they had to give me birth control pills to regulate it. Oh, when I had my first child, I was really a mess, very tired and depressed afterwards. So they put me on antidepressants. I crave sugar and put on weight easily. My digestion isn't very good. And I've had these recurring vaginal yeast problems. But what's this got to do with anything? The doctor has told me there's nothing wrong with me. The tests all came back negative. He says I'm . . ."

I jump in to stop her quoting that litany of negative labels and offer, "I think there may be a physical component to your depression. I don't think all these symptoms are in your head." Mrs. J. bursts into tears of relief.

It's not enough to look at symptoms. It's important to see the pattern and the connection between the symptoms instead of treating each symptom separately.

The challenge is to seek the root cause or causes. A nutritional deficiency? Low thyroid? A suppressed immune system aggravated by allergies or an overgrowth of yeast? Let's consider the last possibility, as many physicians are calling this "the missing diagnosis." An overgrowth of yeast often causes a plethora of health problems but goes undetected and untreated at the source.

Here's a quick look at how the yeast syndrome develops. The human body is teeming with bacteria, viruses and fungi, and billions of friendly germs and antibodies that keep things in balance.

This balance can, however, be upset. When a physician prescribes antibiotics for a bad cold, for example, the purpose is to wipe out the bacteria that may, but usually don't, accompany the cold virus. Antibiotics do not kill the virus. Antibiotics, however, kill off friendly germs, like the intestinal flora. An imbalance is created, and the yeast grows out of control and thus becomes destructive.

This yeast, also known as *Candida albicans,* secretes a toxin into the bloodstream, straining the immune system and weakening our defences. So the old infection comes back. We go to the doctor again. We get more antibiotics, which still don't kill the virus but do kill off more of the friendly bacteria. More yeast grows. And the bacteria are becoming wise to this game.

(A recent report in the *British Medical Journal* concludes, "Prescribing antibiotics for a sore throat does little or no good. And their over-use is helping drug-resistant strains develop." The *New England Journal of Medicine* reports a widespread concern about this overuse of antibiotics. "The danger is that we're becoming more and more vulnerable to drug-resistant super bacteria. And we're running out of antibiotics to treat them.")

The body now attempts to rid itself of this build-up of toxins by secreting them through the skin. The overgrowth and this attempt to purify can contribute to many skin conditions: acne, psoriasis, athlete's foot, rectal itching and fungus under the nails.

The endocrine, or hormonal, system also takes a beating. This can be a factor in chronic fatigue, hormone imbalances, loss of interest in sex, PMS, menstrual problems and infertility. Eventually, in some people, a cascade of illnesses can lead them to feel "sick all over." We haven't developed reliable tests for yeast syndrome, however, and many people, like Mrs. J., are told, "It's all in your head." (Conventional tests often show a false negative.)

Even some psychiatric symptoms may be connected to, or exacerbated by, the yeast syndrome. A Victoria psychiatrist, Abram Hoffer, M.D., has had great success treating emotionally depressed, schizophrenic and even suicidal patients with vitamin therapy and, if they also have yeast symptoms, with an antifungal protocol. After their overall health improves and their yeast symptoms abate, many of the psychiatric problems have also disappeared, or at least improved.

This condition is referred to by several names—Candidiasis Related Syndrome, Chronic Fatigue Syndrome, Myalgic Encephalomyelitis or (erroneously) "Yuppie Flu"—and warrants open-minded research. It is a problem and it is on the increase.

I asked three eminent colleagues, physicians Carolyn Dean, James Balch and Kevin Nolan, who have done extensive research in this field, to set out the treatment plans they have used with their patients. Over the years, I have found their insights very helpful in my health education practice.

A few years ago, David Suzuki, Ph.D., did a CBC television program on this topic and interviewed Carolyn Dean, M.D. She told him that the patients who came to see her, seeking relief from a variety of symptoms, had sometimes seen as many as 20 different specialists. In her book, *Complementary Natural Prescriptions for Common Ailments* (Keats), Dr. Dean summarizes,

Candida Albicans has always lived in the gastro-intestinal tract but under the influence of antibiotics, the birth control pill, cortisone, a highly refined bread and sugar diet, and stress, the yeast are encouraged to overgrow and their toxins and their by-products can adversely affect the whole body.

(Dr. Dean's recommended treatment plan is detailed later in this chapter.) Dr. James Balch's, *Prescription for Nutritional Healing* says:

Because candidiasis can infect various parts of the body—the most common being the ears, nose, gastro-intestinal tract, and bowels—it may manifest as many symptoms including:

- colitis
- abdominal pain
- canker sores
- constipation or diarrhea
- persistent heartburn
- muscle and joint pain
- sore throat
- numbness or tingling sensations
- acne
- vaginitis
- kidney and bladder infections
- arthritis
- depression
- hypothyroidism
- allergies
- sensitivity to the smell of rubber, tobacco, exhaust fumes, perfume and chemical odors.

William Crook, M.D., another pioneer in this field, adds to this already long list:

- Headache
- Fatigue
- Psoriasis
- Asthma
- Autism
- PMS
- Endometriosis
- Multiple sclerosis
- Crohn's disease

The reality is that most physicians are skeptical about this whole topic. Most people with this condition have "made the rounds," at great cost to themselves and to the health care system, and then end up treating themselves. Not something I recommend.

The following is a letter I received in response to a column I wrote:

My wife gave me a copy of *The Yeast Connection* by William Crook, M.D., and I discovered most of the things that I had been suffering from for years were accurately described. Here is a list of my symptoms:
1. Severe migraine headaches beginning in my teens when I had a serious infection that was treated with massive doses of antibiotics;
2. "Fireworks" inside my eyeballs if I flicked my eyes about while keeping [my eyelids] firmly closed;
3. Foot and body odor;
4. Lumps under my skin;
5. Severe athlete's foot, with "cheese" around the nails and skin eaten away as though by acid;
6. Heartburn;
7. Joint pains;
8. Increasing number of allergies;
9. Inexplicable rages;
10. Loud clicking in my ears that coincided with my heart beat;
11. Occasional dizzy spells;
12. Ears constantly getting plugged with excess wax;
13. Severe itching—occasionally I would get the strong sensation that something was "burrowing" just under the skin.

When I described my symptoms to my doctor his reaction was "if I had anything like that I wouldn't tell anybody." He might have been joking, but it wasn't funny. I have been treating myself, following the program in *The Yeast Connection*. ALL of the above conditions are either completely gone or greatly diminished. I'm no longer allergic to wheat, dairy or soy products. No more ear clicking or wax. No more inner light shows. No more dizzy spells. No more athlete's foot. I feel like a new man.

If you have a history of these symptoms, get in touch with a qualified health practitioner familiar with this condition. But be wary of laboratory tests for yeast. I asked Dr. Balch in a recent interview how he tested for chronic fatigue and yeast-related conditions.

Dr. Balch replied,

I don't. There aren't any very reliable tests. It is best to assess people on the basis of their symptoms. Doctors should know the symptoms and the newest treatments. They should listen more to the patient. Candidiasis is a very common problem and multi-factorial. This is one of the reasons that all the people I see are immune depressed to some degree. This is also often linked to stressed adrenal glands.

There are many excellent books. In addition to Dr. Dean's book, the two most useful I have found are *The Yeast Connection and the Woman* by Dr. William Crook (Professional Books)—which also presents excellent information for children and for men—and *Prescription for Nutritional Healing* (the Expanded Edition) by Dr. James Balch and Phyllis Balch.

Dr. Carolyn Dean is a Canadian living in New York, where she is doing clinical research on homeopathic acupuncture for infectious diseases. She recommends this approach for reducing overgrowth of yeast:

1. Cut Out (Down on) Sugar

When making beer or bread, how do you feed the yeast? With sugar. To get rid of your yeast problem, you need to stop feeding it. This is not easy, because the more acute this condition, the more you crave the things that make it worse: sweets and alcohol. When you cut these things out, your symptoms may worsen temporarily as the yeasts die off and release more toxins. This is why I don't recommend doing all of this by yourself. If you have severe symptoms, cut out moldy foods like blue cheese and mushrooms. (The diet recommended in most books can be quite restrictive—no yeasty breads, no fermented vinegar etc. Unless you are severely ill, you probably won't be able to stick to such a restrictive diet.)

2. Replace the Intestinal Flora

The next step is to put the good bacteria back into your body with acidophilus or lactobacillus pills—basically, highly-concentrated yogurt. You can find them at the health food store, in the cooler. It's important to take these on an empty stomach, with a large glass of water. (If you have to be on antibiotics—yes, they do have a vital role—then progressive doctors will prescribe a course of acidophilus capsules *during and after* antibiotics.)

3. Cleanse the System

Most yeast lives in the bowel, which is why diarrhea, constipation and irritable bowel can be related to the yeast syndrome. Eating more fibre—fresh fruit and vegetables and more grains—is helpful. You may also want to move the yeast out with a bulking agent like psyllium—you need to take lots of water when you use this.

4. Boost Your Immune System

(With all the strategies listed in this chapter.)

Most people can do these steps on their own. They are basically good for improving our health. It is wise to work with a skilled health practitioner for the following step.

5. Reduce the Yeast Overgrowth with Antifungal Agents

A natural variety, which is also a natural antibiotic, is garlic. There's a deodorized kind called Kyolic. There are several other natural anti-fungal herbs and an array of prescription drugs. Check with your health practitioner.

Dr. James Balch concurs and offers these recommendations:

1. Try to cut back on the causes. Sugar is a downer and at the top of the list. This is hard because most people with this condition

crave sweet things. Processed foods also depress the immune system and should be avoided.

2. See if it's possible for you to reduce prescription drugs—most drugs depress the immune system. This includes antibiotics, tranquilizers, birth control pills and artificial hormones.

3. Alcohol clobbers the liver which is important in immune health. There may be a craving for alcohol and frequent consumption. You need to cut back.

4. Enhance your immune system with a good diet of fresh whole foods—lots of them raw—and good quality supplements like Vitamin C, grape seed extract...

5. It is very important to replace the natural intestinal flora destroyed by antibiotics with acidophilus capsules.

6. A good antifungal is necessary. Kyolic garlic is the best. Start with one or two and work up to six or eight capsules a day. Local application of the liquid form for skin symptoms is very helpful. Caprylic acid is the next best and can be quite strong. People should realize there may be a reaction when the candida yeast die off. Some physicians prescribe powerful antifungals like nystatin and don't even tell people about the "die off" reaction.

Kevin Nolan, M.D., N.D., a physician and naturopath, advises that conventional tests for a yeast overgrowth aren't reliable.

I don't use them. There are two situations to investigate—first, an overgrowth of yeast; second, an allergy to yeast. In general, anyone who has had a significant overgrowth will develop a yeast allergy. I check this with candida skin allergy testing. And to treat it, I use increasing dilutions of candida.

I don't treat the related conditions until I've treated the yeast overgrowth and allergy because a lot of them, like skin symptoms, a hormone imbalance, neurological problems, even having to get stronger eye glasses, will correct themselves when the yeast overgrowth and allergy have cleared.

I asked Dr. Nolan about antibiotics and he replied, "In my view, antibiotics are needed in less than 10 percent of the time they are prescribed. The Family College of Physicians cautions doctors about their overuse.

Many doctors continue to prescribe because they feel the public demands them."

Dr. Nolan adds, "I will also test for thyroid T3 levels, low iron, magnesium, zinc and B_{12}—blood tests are accurate here. Having treated a yeast overgrowth in the intestinal tract, do not forget to replace the abnormal intestinal flora (bacteria) with healthy acidophilus and bifidus for a month or two, making sure that the digestive pH and nutrition support their growth."

Thyroid T3 is a very new and interesting part of this picture. Physician Denis Wilson describes what he calls Wilson's Syndrome, "a condition that causes symptoms characteristic of decreased thyroid system function." The list of symptoms is extensive and similar to the yeast-related ones; fatigue, headaches, migraine, PMS, fluid retention, anxiety and panic attacks, depression, low sex drive and cold intolerance. To test for this, Dr. Wilson has people take their temperature every morning at the same time, as this condition is characterized by a body temperature that runs on average below normal. The treatment includes T3 supplements—also called Liothyronine—available only by prescription.

As these are very new areas of treatment, your doctor may not be completely up-to-date with them, but I hope he or she will be open to listening to you and reviewing the latest literature.

Finding our way in the maze of a changing health care system is not easy. Of course, we need to take responsibility for our health, but many of us have not felt mainstream medicine has addressed our interest in a more holistic, preventative-oriented, natural medicine. For years, I felt as if I were one of the lone voices in the wilderness, calling out for an approach that embraced the needs of our mind, body and spirit. I'm now encouraged by the growing swell of interest and expertise in what is known as complementary medicine, which integrates conventional and alternative approaches.

Make Healthier Choices

My father is a dentist, and when I was in elementary school in Dallas, he used to come and show us terrible pictures of tongue cancer. They were so horrible that after his talk, we would all make jokes and go out and have a cigarette. That taught me that trying to get people to change out of fear is not very effective . . . So instead of motivating people through the fear of dying, we try to emphasize how a healthier lifestyle can improve the joy of living—the quality and joy within your life, right now.

Dean Ornish, M.D.
in *Healing and the Mind* by Bill Moyers

"Oh, no," I hear you thinking. "This is where she's going to tell me I have to give up everything I like. If I have to exist on brown rice and tofu, I'd rather get sick."

Don't panic! I only want you to make informed choices about what you put in your body. Adopting a healthy lifestyle doesn't mean doing "good" things all the time and avoiding all the "bad" things. It's knowing how some things drain our batteries and others boost them, and making healthier choices *most* of the time.

The following are healthy Type A choices to make throughout your day. Begin to incorporate these as you design your day—as you are ready. Remember, this is a lifelong process, not a goal you're going to knock off this minute.

Waking Up

Open your eyes, yawn and stretch. Lying in bed all night shortens the muscles and stiffens the spine. A one-minute limbering up will gently elongate the muscles and ease your spine into another demanding day of holding you up. My 95-year-old grandfather did daily stretching like this for 60 years and called it "paying the rent." His investment paid off.

In bed, lie on your back and stretch out one arm (above your head) and the opposite leg and hold for 20 seconds; don't forget to breathe. Then stretch the other side. Hold. Then, gently pull your knees up toward your chest, tightening your stomach muscles and bringing your navel in toward your lower back. Hold for 20 seconds. Breathe. This stretching took all of *one minute* and can make all the difference to your back.

As you make your way to the bathroom, breathe deeply and swing your arms. This will help get the blood and *chi* flowing. (A few minutes on a rebounder—a mini trampoline—is excellent for this, when you have time.)

(Unhealthy A's will be brushing their teeth, shaving and rebounding all at once!)

Brushing Your Teeth

Brush with a natural, chemical- and sugar-free toothpaste. You don't need more fluoride, aluminum, sugar—or aspartame, for that matter. Then gently brush your tongue with a few strokes from the back toward the tip. During the night, your system secretes toxins through the skin and through the tongue; you may notice a whitish film on your tongue in the morning. A gentle brush will get rid of these toxins. Then swish with water. Avoid oral antiseptics, mouthwash and hydrogen peroxide: repeated use of these can affect the natural flora and acidity of your saliva.

Showering

Yes, Type A's soak in a tub now and then, but we hit the shower most mornings. Once a week, when you have more time and before you leap into the shower, rub your body *gently* with a dry loofah or a dry natural-bristle brush. A few minutes of brushing your limbs and torso—brush toward the heart—gets circulation and energy flowing and removes toxins that have been secreted by the skin. (Don't do this on your face or other tender areas.) The brush needs to be dry and kept only for this purpose.

Using Deodorant

Most commercial deodorants contain aluminum, which is absorbed through your skin. Choose a deodorant that is made from natural ingredients and that is aluminum-free and perfume-free. Why? Because aluminum may be toxic to your immune and nervous systems. The possible connection between aluminum in the brain and Alzheimer's disease is still being explored, but there are no indications that ingesting aluminum is good for us!

Furthermore, deodorant soaps can be hard on your skin, and most contain harmful additives. Use pure, non-perfumed soaps.

Going Perfume-Free

Virtually all fragrances are petroleum based and hard on the immune system. Aromatherapy and natural herbal oils are not petroleum based and are not toxic. People with chemical sensitivities are like the miner's canary—an early warning to the rest of us. Many people suffer from this, so please consider going perfume-free. I have walked out of shops because of the scented salespeople. (Think of what we could do as a society with the billions of dollars we spend on chemical scents.)

I dearly wish magazine publishers would refuse to insert those perfume and cologne samples in their magazines. I cut them out and throw them away, but the chemicals linger.

Having Breakfast

All right, you don't have time for breakfast. You don't like breakfast. You're not hungry yet. I know. But the fact remains, you need fuel to start up your engine and keep it going until lunch. (Who eats lunch?) Healthy A's know how to make quick pit stops to refuel, and eating breakfast and lunch is essential. Morning is also the time for your beloved coffee or tea. One steaming cup—not the whole pot—will jump-start your system. Now we need some fuel to keep it going.

The High-Fibre Breakfast

There are more benefits to low-fat, high-fibre foods than well-regulated bowels. Fibre in whole grains, legumes, and fruits and vegetables can help control blood cholesterol, and may lower the risk of colon cancer and other cancers. In cool weather, try a steaming bowl of hot whole-grain cereal or warm fruit with room temperature yogurt. In warm weather, have a "sundae" of muesli, high-fibre cold cereal, fresh fruit and yogurt. Garnish with nut flakes. (As you might have guessed, I buy organic cereals sweetened with honey or white grape juice instead of sugar.)

The Rancher's Breakfast

Have an egg and veggie bacon a few times a week. It's best to avoid cured meats such as bacon, sausages and ham, as the nitrates used to preserve them are hard on your immune system and may be a factor in cancer and migraine headaches. My family loves the Yves products. We often eat bacon, deli slices, pepperoni sausage, hot dogs and hamburgers—all made without preservatives, additives or meat. These "meats" are made from tofu, vegetables or grains and are available in health food stores and the more progressive supermarkets.

Fruit Smoothies

If you have no time or no stomach for solid food, a blender is invaluable. Throw in a banana, some yogurt and whatever else looks good. Blend while you're making your first sales calls, if you like; drink some now or take it in a mug or Thermos for later. Even better, make this a power drink with the immune boosters from Step 6.

Carrying a Snack Pack

Take some healthy munchies, such as little boxes of raisins, some trail mix or a banana, to work. Take a Thermos filled with a power drink or fruit juice. Carry a water bottle and sip frequently. In the mid-morning, dip into your snack pack. Skip the cheese danish. Skip the croissant. Pastries may look light but are packed with fat you don't need. Also, beware of most commercial muffins. They can contain as much fat and sugar as any cupcake. Although your brain needs glucose to operate, please don't resort to candy bars or colas. Your blood sugar likes to be maintained at a fairly even level. When you don't eat breakfast or lunch and you're tearing around, burning up fuel, your blood sugar gets low and you feel tired and hungry. Candy or a cola might seem to offer an energy boost, but such choices backfire, shooting your blood sugar level way up, and the insulin rush then drops it lower than it was before.

Sugar and Your Immune System

Guess how many teaspoons of sugar there are in a cola. Ten! Can you imagine taking ten teaspoons of sugar in your coffee? Ginger ale has 8 teaspoons. Your average chocolate shake contains 12 teaspoons of sugar and a whopping 14 grams of fat.

Instead of a soda why not make your own sparkling fruit juice? White grape juice and mineral water makes a great drink. Some fizzy bottled fruit drinks are better than regular soda pop, which is made with sugar or aspartame, water, chemicals, caffeine, artificial colouring and artificial flavouring. But non-fizzy, unsweetened fruit juice is even better. Read the labels: fructose is better than sucrose; uncarbonated is better than carbonated.

We have known for some time that sugar is bad for our teeth. New research suggests it also weakens our immune system. Nutritionist Ann Gittlemen, author of *Cut the Sugar Out* (Crown), offers more than you ever wanted to know about the effects of your favourite sweets:

1. Proven to destroy the germ-killing ability of white blood cells for up to five hours after ingesting.
2. Reduces production of antibodies, proteins that combine with and inactivate foreign invaders in the body.
3. Interferes with the transport of vitamin C.
4. Causes mineral imbalances and sometime allergic reactions and makes cells more permeable to invasion by allergens and microorganisms.

The immune system is so sensitive to sugars of all kinds that its effectiveness is reduced to half when sugars are consumed. Sugar also elevates blood triglyceride levels, hastens the fat-storage process, wildly imbalances blood sugar and causes tooth decay.

I don't like hearing this stuff either, if it makes you feel any better. But I'd rather know about this so that if my immune system feels weak—I feel tired or I have the first signs of a cold or flu—I know to stay away from all sugars. Another nutritionist, Rosie Schwartz, author of *The Enlightened Eater* (Macmillan Canada), tells us that we may be eating as many as three teaspoons of sugar with our breakfast cereal, and that's before we add any sugar. (I once read a report that said there was better nutrition in the cardboard box than in the sugar-coated cereal inside.)

To boost health, get energy and keep blood sugar levels in balance, skip the candy bar and stoke your engines with a healthier, and more lasting, fuel like half a sandwich, a few almonds, a banana or yogurt.

Remembering to Eat Lunch

Yes, I know you don't often have time for a leisurely lunch, but fast food doesn't have to be junk food, and you can make healthier choices almost anywhere. A clear soup is better than a cream one; a salad is better than fries; an olive oil dressing is better than a creamy one; pan-fried food is better than deep-fried; and steamed is better than pan-fried. I always ask for my dressing or sauce on the side; then I can add only a bit. Try to eat raw vegetables and fresh fruit every day.

Drinking Good Water

There is nothing better for your body than a drink of pure water. However, it's a rare part of the world that still has unpolluted water. You may want to consider installing a filter. Drinking pure water—at least six glasses a day or, as Dr. James Balch recommends, one glass every few hours you're awake—is essential to maintaining the proper functioning of your system. We must have water for everything from flushing out wastes to keeping our skin clear. Regular tea and coffee don't count, as they increase urination. Keep a bottle of filtered water on your desk and carry one in your car.

Our system likes to maintain an even keel. When it is warm outside, it's great to drink cool drinks. When it is cool outside, it's good to drink warm drinks. One winter, when my father was in hospital trying to fight off a resistant pneumonia infection, it grieved me to see the well-meaning nurses handing out ice water—not helpful in winter, particularly when you're fighting an infection. Iced drinks inhibit the secretion of digestive enzymes. So when you go into a restaurant, why is ice water the first thing they bring you and coffee the second? Because most of our choices are not smart; they have been driven by taste and by marketing ploys—not by health.

Recharging with a Quick Snooze

One day, I was in the outer office of a very successful executive, waiting to meet with him. I was told he was with someone, but before I was shown in, no other person came out. In our conversation, he offered that he had been taking a nap, something he did every day after lunch, for 20 minutes. There's a good reason why we feel like napping after lunch: it's part of our body's natural rhythm. A short rest (not long enough to disturb your night-time sleep) will recharge your batteries and refuel your tank. As he explained it,

> I work long hours and I work hard. I make a lot of decisions around here and my mind needs to be clear. This break enables me to have two days in one. After my forty winks, I feel as fresh as if it's a new day.

I wondered about his assistant, out there at the front desk, so I asked him. "Well, I've even got her taking a power nap during her coffee break in the afternoon."

That go-getter you know who seems to have boundless energy and health may be sneaking a snooze. Can you find a way to work this healthy A asset into your day?

Recharging Mid-Afternoon

When you feel low on energy, dip into your snack pack with the fruit, power drink and raisins. If you like to have a coffee after lunch, make it a decaf. Believe it or not, many people become sensitized to caffeine and find their afternoon coffee break keeps them from getting to sleep at night.

Recharging at the End of the Day

I once remarked to a seminar group, "There should be a place where we can release some steam after work before we have to hit the home scene." A participant offered, "There is. It's called a bar."

Or you might try—
• Sitting and doing some of your belly breathing
• Having a quick nap when you get home

- Getting outside and walking around a few blocks
- Putting on some music and dancing around your house

If the word exercise scares you, just think of it as "active living."

Ten Best Reasons Not to Exercise

1. No time. I'm much too busy.
2. Too much effort.
3. It's boring.
4. Too expensive.
5. I've got a bad back.
6. I'm too tired. I'm beat. No energy left. Sorry.
7. I'm just too lazy. Not one of those go-getter types. I really prefer to lie here.
8. It gives me a headache. And I hate all that jumping up and down.
9. I've just eaten. It's not good to run around on a full stomach.
10. Why bother? I'm never going to be really fit.

Try These Strategies

1. Make time. If you can find the time to flop in front of the TV for a couple of hours a night, you can find the time to exercise.
2. Once you get started, it'll get easier. You'll have more energy and get sick less often. And you'll sleep better, too.
3. Choose an activity you enjoy. Running may be boring, but how about a community badminton or volleyball class? Go cycling with your kids. You're smart; you can find something fun.
4. It doesn't have to be expensive. Walking is one of the best health boosters, and it is free, as is dancing in wild abandon around your living room.
5. Exercise can help your back. Don't go for the world sit-up record, but firming up your stomach muscles is the best thing for your back. If your back is in really bad shape, join a Healthy Back program at the YMCA or YWCA or at your local recreation centre.
6. Exercise gives you energy. Really busy people often find they couldn't handle the pace and pressure without exercising.
7. You can choose not to be lazy. No one is saying you have to become a marathon runner; simply decide that you don't want to live the rest of your life as a slug.

8. If vigorous exercise bothers you, find something more soothing, with an easier pace. How about yoga? It's a good way to strengthen your muscles and relax. (More on this in Step 9.)
9. You can go for a walk in the evening. After supper, my husband and I often go for a stroll.
10. But you can be fitter. Find something you enjoy and make it fun.

Delighting in Dining

Lest you think I'm a complete spoilsport, bad-mouthing your favourite things, here are a few *positive* suggestions:

- Try my better butter. Take half a pound of pure unsalted, uncoloured butter—it's in the freezer in your grocery store—and let it come to room temperature. Blend it in a food processor with one-third to one-half of a cup of cold-pressed, light olive oil. (Experiment with the proportions.) This spread is low in salt and has no chemicals, colouring or preservatives. Olive oil may help reduce cholesterol and is one of the health-giving secrets in the Mediterranean diet.
- Buy non-hydrogenated margarine. It is better than regular hydrogenated, which has more unhealthy saturated fat. As you may know, there are good fats and bad fats. The bad guys are found mostly in red meat and dairy products. The good guys, mostly in vegetable oils, fish oils and nuts.
- Opt for canola oil when it's available; it has the least amount of saturated fat.
- Try meatless meals more often. Tofu is a great source of low-fat protein; it is bland by itself but very tasty when seasoned with, for example, garlic and black bean sauce. And soy products contain a substance similar to estrogen that may reduce the risk of breast cancer and that many women say eases some of the symptoms of menopause.
- My family prefers non-dairy milk. I buy a blend of organic soy and rice milk. Some soy milk brands taste chalky and awful. Ask the natural foods manager to suggest a good one. If you want to drink cow's milk and you're not allergic to it, make it skim or 2 percent.
- Tofu hot dogs are a lot healthier than pork or beef hot dogs, which are usually high in fat and full of nitrates and other preservatives.
- Soy cheese is a good substitute for regular cheese. Make pizzas with whole-wheat crusts, vegetable toppings and a sprinkling (not an inch-thick layer) of soy cheese.

- Wash fruits and vegetables before eating, to remove pesticide residues and wax. All non-organic fruit is sprayed and waxed; sometimes it's even shellacked! None of these substances should be in your body. Run these fruits and vegetables under the hot water tap before eating. You can buy a product at the natural food store that will rinse off most of the coatings and additives. (It takes only one minute to rinse.)
- Grow, buy and eat organic whenever you can. And it's better not to use animal manure on your vegetable garden lest you pick up some parasites.
- Eat more fish; its omega-3 oils are thought to lower cholesterol. Bake, broil, poach, sauté—don't deep-fry. Some people feel that farm salmon are not as healthy as the wild type, but wild salmon is not that easy to get. Deep-sea fish, which swim in less polluted waters than those closer to shore, are best. Shellfish is high in cholesterol and often full of industrial toxins, depending on its origin, so eat it only occasionally and make sure you know where it comes from.
- Eat more beans and other high-fibre foods including multi-grain bread. The heavier the bread, the healthier it is. Avoid white bread, which is low in fibre. (Remember in kindergarten the recipe for glue? White flour and water.)
- Eat lots of garlic; it's a powerful natural antibiotic and anti-fungal that stimulates the immune system. Recent studies indicate it may prevent cancer.
- Try quinoa and other grains such as millet and barley; they are an interesting and healthy change from potatoes, rice or noodles. Couscous is very handy for the Type A cook; it's a quick-cooking cereal popular in Middle Eastern cooking.
- Enjoy more steamed vegetables, fresh foods, raw foods and salads. Eat cruciferous vegetables—foods from the cabbage family, including broccoli. These are cancer-fighting foods.
- Watch that salad dressing—one of the biggest sources of fat in the North American diet.
- Frequent vegetarian restaurants.
- Go to the library or bookstore and check out cookbooks from the Mediterranean, Middle Eastern and Asian countries where cuisine is based largely on grains, vegetables and interesting flavours.

Avoiding MSG

Monosodium glutamate (MSG) is a flavour enhancer that is often used in Asian restaurants and in many of our canned and prepared foods and that causes allergic reactions in many people. It has been known to cause headaches, tightness in the chest, diarrhea, and nervous system and brain disorders. Some scientists suspect large amounts could harm an unborn child. Soups are usually heavily laced with MSG to make them more tasty with fewer real ingredients—a chicken broth without MSG would require many more chickens. MSG is found in Ac'cent, meat tenderizers and most seasoning sauces. Read the labels. It may be listed as *natural flavouring, hydrolyzed plant protein or hydrolyzed vegetable protein.*

Enjoying a Drink

Please use alcohol sparingly. Alcohol masquerades as a relaxant, but it's really a depressant. It's not helpful for treating stress or helping you sleep. Alcohol has a rebound effect, so that even if it mellows you out initially, it will agitate you later. Yes, have a glass of wine with dinner, or a drink at a party. But look for organic wines with fewer pesticides, and at the bottle-it-yourself wine store you get wine made without sulphites. A nip now and then may even be good for us, but we need to be mindful about what we're nipping and how often.

Going to Bed

If you like to watch the evening news, it's better to do it earlier than just before you go to sleep. You're better off without the electric blanket or an electric clock by your ear, or the television too close because of the electromagnetic fields. Many physicians advise their pregnant patients not to use electric blankets, particularly during the first few months, as there's evidence electromagnetism may be a factor in miscarriages. Research into the effects of electromagnetic fields on human health is still inconclusive, but many scientists believe there's enough reason to be cautious about long-term exposure.

Many unhealthy A's have problems sleeping and need the rest to recharge. Insomnia is one of the most common disorders in North America, affecting almost a quarter of the adult population. Chronically tired people have more accidents, and get sick more often. Deep, restful, drug-free sleep is essential. Researchers report that repairing the immune system may be one of the main functions of sleep.

Sleeping pills are a bad idea. Not only are they addictive, but most of them will eventually make insomnia worse by disrupting the normal sleep cycle. But here are a few natural methods that can help:

- Try herbal products. While not as strong as prescription drugs, they can be very effective. Valerian, for one, is quite strong. Check the selection in your natural food store.
- Drink herbal "sleepy time" teas with a bit of honey or a cup of hot milk before bed.
- Take calcium or magnesium supplements.
- Reduce your caffeine intake; more than a couple of cups early in the day might be affecting your sleep, even if they never have before.
- Make your bedroom comfortable, dark and quiet, and don't use the bed for doing work.
- Go to bed and get up at roughly the same times each day. Your body will get used to the pattern.
- Exercise earlier in the day. This burns off the adrenalin that keeps your brain churning.
- Do the relaxation exercises you learned in this book.

Please take action if you are not sleeping well.

The questionnaire on the following page will guide you in taking action in other areas and will help you prioritize. It's not an exam. Please be realistic and start with the easier challenges.

I sincerely hope you do not feel overwhelmed by all of the details, many of them dire, in the last few steps. Nobody's expecting you to examine every mouthful before eating it, or to be so neurotic about your choices that you can't enjoy your life. I just want you to be informed. What you do with this information is up to you. Even making a few changes to maximize your credits and reduce some debits can yield big benefits in becoming a healthy Type A.

I don't lead a perfect life. But whenever possible, I try to eat fresh, organic fruits and vegetables. I eat fewer meat and dairy products and more fish and whole grains. I drink lots of pure water. I take my green power drink every morning. I use natural cosmetics and live as chemically free as I can. I watch less TV and listen to more CBC radio. I snack on nuts and seeds instead of chips. I get out for brisk walks. I muck about in the garden. I spend meaningful time with good friends. I listen to music that makes the soul soar.

I enjoy making healthier choices. And so can you!

The Lifestyle Action Plan

Taking Stock

My current health challenge(s): _____

To meet this challenge I will: _____

_____

Decreasing Debits

Caffeine: Current score mg @ day _____ Objective _____

Another lifestyle debit to minimize:

_____

Boosting Credits

1. A way to get fit that I enjoy: _____

Another lifestyle credit to increase:

_____

My habitual way of making changes: _____

_____

A more effective strategy to get going and keep on track:

_____

Why bother? My motivation is: _____

_____

To boost my energy and immune system I am going to:

_____

To have more fun in my life I am going to:

_____

Transform Your Critic into a Coach

It's the support and care and love that you give yourself that gives you the real strength to care for and love others.

Oprah Winfrey
A Journal of Daily Renewal

I once asked a group, "What do you need to be a good coach?" A fellow called out cheerily, "You need a minivan." Well, yes, but after the minivan you need to be a good motivator.

We can learn new life skills, but these will only take us so far unless we're able to nurture our greatest potential asset: a positive attitude.

Our inner coach encourages us to do our best, but assures us that winning is not everything, that winning is not about proving our worth. The skillful inner coach inspires us to connect with our basic goodness and innate confidence. It tells us we can have fun and goof off sometimes—without feeling guilty. It allows us to make mistakes and learn from them, instead of beating ourselves up.

Many of us grew up with an inner critic that was harsh and judgemental, and that critic has undermined our confidence. The important thing to remember is where that voice comes from; it is the culmination of years of conditioning by our society, our families and the people around us.

No blame. Our parents were trying to do their best for us—their best as they saw it. "Work as hard as you can. Be the best. Get ahead. Excel. Win. I want to be proud of you. Why can't you be like your brother and sister? You're never going to make it in this world." Their words and actions may have built us up or torn us down. Whatever the tone, these early experiences, or imprints have shaped our values, our work ethics, our sense of responsibility, our way of relating to others, and to a large degree our way of seeing ourselves. They have had a great impact on the nature of our inner critic and inner coach.

As we grow up, we come to believe in other people's visions of ourselves and lose sight of our own basic nature. We find ourselves living out others' expectations, rather than our own. And these reactions arise from this early conditioning.

If we had a lot of unconditional love and support from our parents, this will boost our self-confidence. And this foundation will always be there for us; it is a great gift. We may, however, go overboard in our drive to excel—we want so much for them to be proud of us. Our confidence may swell to arrogance. We may feel so proud that we are critical and scornful of "lesser" beings. Our sharp minds may become judgemental critics. This negative voice may chastise us or others when we fail to hit the highest mark.

If our early years were more harsh, we may carry a lack of confidence and feel that our self-worth is based on our performance. "I am worthy as long as I am achieving, as long as I'm getting things done." This script is at the root of many "workaholic" A's. As soon as we deviate from the script, we feel guilty. The inner critic can rule our lives and manifest itself as difficulty in trusting others, fear and reluctance to show our vulnerability, difficulty in establishing loving relationships, and increased anger.

Hostility—The Hallmark of the Unhealthy Type A

The term *Type A* was coined as a synonym for free-floating hostility. "Easily angered" always topped the list of our traits. (This got us even hotter under the collar!)

Research on Type A behaviour led to Type A's being labelled "hot reactors." And this aspect was isolated as the main coronary risk factor by Redford Williams, M.D., and his researchers at Duke University. (In his excellent book, *The Trusting Heart* (Random House), Dr. Williams advises, "The antidote to hostility is to develop a more trusting heart.")

This connection between hostility and the heart is not new. In 1628, the English physician William Harvey wrote with great insight, "We are at the mercy of any person who might want to anger us. This affection of the mind is the cause of an agitation whose influence extends to the heart."

Daniel Goleman, Ph.D., is the author of the best seller *Emotional Intelligence* (Bantam Books) and writes for the *New York Times*. (He has reviewed the literature in this area in great depth.) In an article in the *New York Times Magazine*, he summarized the results of a number of studies:

> People who are chronically hostile, who see the world through a lens of suspicion and cynicism, are particularly vulnerable to heart disease. The data also suggest that hostility increases the risk of contracting a range of other ailments as well. By the same token, amiability—plain old good naturedness—seems to have a protective effect on health.

Yes, we A's can exude that good naturedness. We have it in us. And softening our inner critic and quelling our quick temper help us reveal our goodness. Being easily angered is not our basic nature. Our high-spirited, quick-to-react style makes us susceptible to acting as hot reactors, but this tendency can be tamed. The general view of us has been quite fixed—for example, we are aggressive and lack gentleness—but no one's behaviour is one-sided. Yes, we do have fiery energy that can manifest itself as anger, but that fire can also surface as personal warmth, when we allow it to radiate. So let's take a close look at how and why we bristle so easily and what we can do about this.

The Dalai Lama is an inspiring example of the pacification of anger. Although he lost his homeland and a million Tibetans lost their lives, he regards the invaders with compassion, not anger.

> As a destructive force there is nothing as strong as anger. It upsets our physical equilibrium and disturbs our rest. Happiness, peace and sleep evade us, and we can no longer appreciate people who have helped us and deserve our trust and gratitude . . .
>
> Whenever we think about someone who has wronged us or who is doing something we don't want, our mind feels unsettled. This state of mind fuels our negative thoughts, "what a nasty person," and our anger grows stronger and stronger. It is at the stage of the unsettled feeling we should step in.

There are two opposite views of dealing with anger: one is to ventilate; the other is to repress. In the ventilation approach, we're supposed to get it "off our chest." At the other extreme, repression can be so effective, we may not even be aware of the seething energy that eats away within us. Both approaches have drawbacks.

There is, as ever, a middle way. Although I spent a good many years working with Gestalt and other therapeutic group methods, I am not an advocate of freely expressing anger. I've seen too much harm inflicted through outbursts of anger. Words have power. Words can hurt. Words cannot be taken back. We need to be mindful of their effect.

We may feel temporarily unburdened by our outburst, but what about the other person? We have exorcised our negativity but if we have just dumped it on someone else, not only will this hurt them, but it will come back to us. And giving our anger free rein can become a habitual pattern, we can even get hooked on the adrenalin of being fired up all the time.

In addition, being a hot reactor can become a habitual feature of our personality—a bad habit. As you may know from painful experience, this feature is a great drawback in relating to others. If we fear that our parent, our partner, our boss or our friend is angry and may lash out at any minute, it is very hard to open up to him or her.

Keeping anger bottled up is not the answer either. Many studies report the ill effects of repressing our anger (we don't need studies to tell us this, though). Repressed anger can be a factor in gastro-intestinal conditions, heart disease and even cancer. And carrying around resentments under-mines our relationships. We cannot be open and caring if we are bearing hostility.

In my experience, if we allow ourselves to look a bit deeper into the anger, we find a layer of stored resentments, another layer of old hurts and then an underlying layer of fear. Our anger may be serving as a protective cocoon. It can feel much safer to bristle than to feel the rawness of our vul-nerability.

As healthy A's we develop the emotional bravery to see through these layers and transmute the destructive energy of anger into the constructive energy of compassion. How? Cooling down, as we learned in Step 4, and acquiring the mindfulness and awareness that are presented in the Step 9 are the best solutions I know for this challenge.

When I was growing up, both my parents were loving coaches and often were frustrated with my brothers and me, but they rarely, if ever, expressed any anger. When we were upset by an injustice or conflict, my mother coun-selled us, "If you knew the agony in the other person's soul." I used to balk at this. In my childish way, I wanted someone to make the offender pay for being mean to me.

But I have come to see that empathy is a useful way to diffuse anger. When someone is irritating you, try looking beyond the behaviour. (A fault-finding person makes us so mad.) It's easy to lash out in defensive anger.

However, what if we were to shift our state of mind into that of the coach? What if we were able to generate some compassion based on seeing the other person's struggle? Is this person insecure and seeking to bolster him- or herself by tearing us down? Can we feel a soft spot in our hearts for him or her? This is great practice for us. Generating compassion is quite profound and the foundation of genuine spiritual realization. My mother also used to remind us, "Anyone can love someone who is easy to love; the challenge is to love a difficult person." And if we reflect on this advice, we see that a difficult person is someone who probably really needs our love. At the core of all the difficult people I've ever known, there was a strong dose of self-loathing. Seeing this has helped me feel compassion for them. Combining these practices with the physical cooling down of Step 4 is very helpful. The temperature gauge on our dashboard is there to remind us when we're getting overheated.

Recently, when I was beginning to steam about a hassle with which my husband and I were confronted, he leaned over to me and offered, "Why don't you try one of your little exercises?" A sense of humour helps, too.

An overdeveloped critic can manifest itself as anger or as a chronically negative attitude. We can easily become mired in a swamp of negative thoughts and beliefs. With hearts full of grief, we lose sight of more positive ways of being.

Eventually, being lost in negativity and incapable of letting judgemental thoughts go becomes a way of being and can turn into depression. There are many other components to depression, including low *chi* and a compromised immune system, but self-loathing and a gloomy outlook bring dark clouds. It doesn't have to be this way.

Oranges or Lemons?

I have culled a lot of wisdom from taxi drivers over the years. One explained why he was so cheerful on a rainy November day: "Every morning you have a choice. You can put a bit of sour lemon or a bit of sweet orange in your mouth, and this will flavour your whole day." This is a great example of what it is like having the critic or the coach at the wheel.

Sideline Critics

Some years ago a group asked me to assist them getting a project off the ground. It was something that I believed in, so I was happy to help. The group was dedicated but lacked a plan and was quite disorganized. People were great at talking about doing things, but not that great at actually doing those things.

Before long my natural "take charge" energy was taking charge. The group asked me to take the lead. I worked tirelessly to make this project a success, which it was. Then I overheard a couple of the people criticizing me. "She always thinks she has to be the one in charge."

I was hurt. It seemed unfair: I had volunteered a lot of time. When I recovered, I asked myself, "Even though I still think I was unfairly criticized, what can I learn?"

This situation and many situations like it have been instrumental in my development as a healthy Type A. Yes, people welcome a doer into their midst, but then criticize from the sidelines; this approach is much easier than risking centre field. Again, this was an opportunity to rouse my compassion. I imagined it was inner negativity that undermined the willingness of these people to step forward and take on some of the responsibility and some of the risk. Their criticizing was not coming from a place of inner richness.

Recently, I volunteered to help with another project, and it went quite differently. When asked to chair the meetings, I declined—even I'm learning to say no now and then. And instead of trying to hog the limelight with my bright ideas, I was more interested in being of genuine assistance—working in the background and letting others feel empowered. It felt good to be a sideline coach.

Over the years, my awareness has improved enough to enable me to sense earlier my forcefulness; I can now detect when I'm beginning to get off balance. Jumping in to override someone's idea by changing the direction of the conversation to *my* direction and feeling pressure to grab the wheel happen less and less. Things flow more smoothly if I'm less interested in myself and more interested in others and the success of the project.

This shift is important. On occasion, we A's can be a tad self-absorbed. So stepping out with less criticism, less hostility and more warmth is the key to our becoming healthy A's.

When we can be assertive *and* spacious, sharp and soft, we are developing genuine power.

One way to do this is to reframe the negative self-talk of the critic into the encouragement of the coach. (Remember, our nervous system, our immune system, our whole body overhears and reacts to the tone and words of our inner dialogue so calming self-talk will ease our stress considerably, as well.)

Please read though these reminders and repeat them to yourself. Then apply liberally throughout the day.

Coach Reminders

Pause • Tune in • Breathe • Gear down • Relax • Let go
Slow down • Cool down • Sit back • Step back • Listen
It's not that important • Don't panic
Take a break • Go for a walk • Stretch those muscles
Expect obstacles as part of every process
Be kind • I don't need to dance to that old tune
Don't be so hard on myself • I can say "No"
Do what I can and let go of the rest
Have some fun
This is workable
This is not a life or death emergency • Be calm
This will take some time • Be patient
All done in good time • Be gentle
Take things as they come
I don't need to proclaim myself
I don't need to prove I'm right
I don't need to win at everything
I don't need to be jealous
I can appreciate what I've got and not fixate on what I haven't
I don't need to dominate every situation
I don't need to talk all the time
I can be a leader and a team player
I can choose to be irritated or at ease
I choose not to have unrealistic expectations
I choose not to live according to others' expectations
I can choose to be happy or sad
Down time is time well spent
It is good to take time to recharge
Guilt is a waste of energy
I can choose to let go of guilt
That's old stuff—Let it go
That's not a reality yet—Let it go
Don't regret the past or fear the future
Life has its ups and downs: this is an up—it will pass; this is a down—it will pass
See the good in others
Appreciate more than criticize
Everything changes • Nothing is permanent
Being is as important as doing
Be here now • Savour the moment
This moment is all there is
Do something meaningful for this world

Jot down the phrases that speak to you. And post them where you'll see them. At your desk? On the fridge?

Transforming the Critic into an Inner Coach

This an ongoing process. We don't have to talk to ourselves all the time. But when we hear that nagging voice, we can turn it around, transmuting the negative energy into positive.

In this way, it is possible to retrain ourselves into a more positive frame of mind. In its formal form, this process is called "cognitive therapy," but it doesn't necessarily require professional services, unless a person is in a serious depression. It's much like the way we've discussed dealing with stressful situations.

However, this retraining is not merely putting on a happy face; it's learning to change our thinking patterns so that they are more healthy—and more realistic. The proponents of the power of positive thinking tell us that people who begin consciously to modify their inner conversations and assumptions report an almost immediate improvement in their performance, their energy and their contentment.

This new ground may feel unsettling at first (sometimes sticking with familiar grudges feels less frightening than taking a leap of faith into the unknown), but there is great potential in finding a more positive way of being.

Frank—A Second Chance

In this program, Frank, the older fellow from the cardiac clinic, discovered a whole new side of himself. I could see the light in his eyes come alive again. Frank turned out to be quite a cheerful fellow.

Frank had been buried under layers of other people's expectations. He developed great insight.

I've worked hard my whole life and I thought I was successful. When I came so close to death I realized that I hadn't been happy. I was running flat out in a life that didn't have much meaning. I got all riled up over every little thing. I had lost touch with my wife and our kids. Now, when the whole family gets together, we talk and really listen to each other. And not about the weather or sports, like we used to. We talk from the heart like we do here in our group. It feels good. That heart attack was the best thing that ever happened to me. It woke me up.

As much as I'd like you to have this awakening, I don't recommend waiting for a heart attack or positive results from a biopsy.

Marie—Quieting the Inner Critic

Marie didn't have a sudden jolt. Her realization was a slow dawning.

> I see now why I kept so busy. It kept me from really feeling how lonely I was and grieving over my mother's death. I was so focused on making my mark. I guess I'm still trying to please my father, even though he died years ago. Besides, there was no pleasing him. It seems that just being aware of those old voices has helped loosen their grip. Now when I hear that chastising critic, "Marie if you were more organized, then you'd be able to take that on," I realize it's never enough. And trying to be perfect at everything is not in line with my heart's desires. You helped me realize that all of this striving to be the best at everything was contributing to my loneliness. I was so competitive I alienated my colleagues at work, and even the men I dated. I was so driven I didn't make time for friends, and dismissed people so easily. I missed a lot.

These insights were painful for Marie. She saw that she had spent her life struggling to attain goals that were not in line with what was going to make her happy. Her inner critic came down on her for this, and she felt she must make some radical changes. She was relieved when I suggested that she didn't need to abandon her business and retreat to the "simple life" in the backwoods. With some minor adjustments here and there, we can work with our lives as they are. It's quite possible to be busy and at ease, to be successful in the outer world and fulfilled in the inner one. We can have a thriving spiritual side and a thriving business.

Marie made great strides when she focused her mind on the challenges within.

> I never really spent much time with myself—being quite the extrovert—but I do appreciate what the meditation and relaxation have done. More awareness is really the key. Now I am able to see and let go of those old negative scripts and turn them around. I am appreciating little everyday things.

Last weekend I was outside working in the garden and noticed the lovely wooden bench that I'd discovered at a garage sale. It struck me that I never sit on it. So I did. I just sat there soaking in the sights and smells of the roses. Up pops the inner grouch with "Why are you wasting time? There's so much to do." I just laughed. I feel so free now I no longer have to dance to that tune.

Kim and Aaron—Working Together

It took some time for Kim, the scientist who came to this country several years ago, to see how deeply her parents and culture had instilled in her a driven inner critic that was obsessed with achieving. In our discussions, she sorted out which aspects of her scripts were useful to her now and which were not. Like Marie, she did not have to quit her job to find the contentment for which she longed.

Kim did, however, need to make some changes. While she liked being a person who could be counted on, she was very tired of doing so much. But when she let up, her inner critic would scold her and she'd feel guilty. She had to remind herself that this one-sided life was no longer what she wanted. Learning to say no and setting boundaries were major steps for her.

The inner coach would encourage her to speak her mind. "I really would love to be able to help you out with that work, but to be honest, I don't have the time to do it justice. Thank you for the invitation, but I have to say no."

Aaron, the go-getter realtor she dated, shared these challenges. So much of his life had been dictated slavishly by this creed: I have to be number one; anything less is failure.

In our sessions, he saw that even when he did win at something, it was a hollow victory. He realized that he felt better and got along much better with others when he was not trying to beat them at everything. (His idea of time off had been trying to defeat his co-workers at golf.) Aaron discovered a kind of ease that came from sitting back once in a while and letting others take the lead. Not feeling pressured to prove himself all the time seemed to make him feel more confident inside. (One of the myths about Type A's is that because we make such convincing noises, we are brimming with inner confidence.) Aaron still worked long hours, still made the "President's Club," but he could pause and share a joke. He also turned out to be quite funny and made Kim laugh with his dry wit. This helped her open up more. They became a team.

Kim and Aaron married and discovered how stressful combining a family can be. Kim, particularly, found it trying. Now, she and Aaron had four children—none of whom seemed to get along. Kim wondered why she had complained about being stressed before. This was a true test of the insight she'd gained and the skills she'd learned.

She talked things out with Aaron. She told Aaron that they had to be clear with each other and set aside time for the whole family to be together and time just for themselves. She also talked with the children, insisting that everyone help with the house cleaning on Saturday morning. Kim hired a teenage neighbour to babysit the children after school, do some laundry and make supper. The babysitter is happy to have the extra income, and the arrangement makes juggling the home and work plates easier for Kim and Aaron.

As Kim remarked,

> Before I came to see you, I would have tried to do it all. It would have been very hard for me to admit that I couldn't do it all. Now, I see there is no reason. Why should I do all the work at home my mother did and try to have a successful career like my father? I have to keep turning those negative phrases into positive ones, because that goading voice is pretty convincing. But I feel so much freer when I just don't listen to it.
>
> Letting go of these inner pressures has enabled Aaron and me to cut back: we're letting some of the other parents take a turn at organizing the baseball games; our children are not in so many extra activities—that was more from our ambition for them to be high achievers. We still want them to do well, but we want them to balance this with being happy within themselves. Some of our friends are frantic, they are all so booked up, even the young children, with so many classes and sports.

Kim and Aaron are designing their lives creatively. They are no longer just reacting to their lives—they're living them more consciously.

Lest You Think of Me as a Paragon of Virtue...

"How do *you* deal with pressure?" I'm often asked.

Sorry to say, getting a Ph.D. in psychology didn't endow me with a kit of miraculous solutions. What I've learned as a person, in my forty-something years, is more of a process than a prescription. It's not about mastering techniques; it's about making shifts in viewing life and viewing myself, reassessing goals and priorities, and developing my inner coach. Mostly, it seems to be a journey of letting go.

Letting go of self-imposed pressure has been very helpful. I used to be much more concerned about how I was seen by others. At first, I even made a concentrated effort to sound knowledgeable, to sound like an "academic," which I am not. Fortunately, that insecurity was lost long ago.

Speaking simply from the heart, rather than like an expert, feels better. I like to think that people still see me as reasonably credible, but there's much less concern about how others see me. I have also decided that I don't need to be the perfect wife, the perfect mother, the perfect professional. Having fewer expectations has eased the pressure and released a lot of energy.

Letting go of trying to run every show was also helpful. Being blessed, or burdened, with a strong mind, I felt the need to control things, and too often was able to get away with it.

I remember sitting in an agonizingly slow meeting—a true Type A torture. People were gabbing away and not getting on with the agenda. Tugging at the leash, my impatient inner critic wanted them to get to the point so I could polish off this event and get on to the next. Hurry up! was my mantra.

This is where my coach stepped in. I realized that my frustration was that they weren't getting on with *my* agenda. My goal-oriented mind wanted to see something concrete happen. The others wanted to get to know each other first—to bond. So, I took a few deep breaths, sat back and let go. Then I rather enjoyed the chatter.

Letting go is also about respect. Your way of doing something may be different than mine, and just as good. What is true for me may not be true for you. Allowing space for others to be who they are, rather than who I want them to be, lessens the pressure on us all.

Letting Go Is a Choice

When we shift into a more positive mode and open ourselves to the possibility of letting go, there are many opportunities.

In the following scenarios, the critic usually goes for the first option; the coach, for the second:

Option A. It's not the right table. The waiter has shown you to the wrong table. You had your eye on that one, over there by the window. You protest.

"Sorry, that's reserved," you're informed. You sulk. Who is responsible for the spoiled evening? The waiter? The people who claim *your* table? The table? Perhaps, it's your critic's reluctance to let go?

Option B. While you would rather have sat by the window, you accept the table that is available. Before long you have settled in. You chat with your companion, you sip some wine, and soon you have forgotten all about the table. It's a delightful evening.

Option A. Your boss doesn't respect you. Some days this bugs you. Some days it infuriates. Why doesn't he acknowledge your expertise? Why doesn't he consider your views? His cool dismissal begins to affect your performance. You begin to turn his criticism inwards on yourself.

Option B. Your boss doesn't respect you. Actually, you don't respect him much either. He's not good at managing people. But you choose not to be thrown off. When you hear yourself mutter about his lack of sensitivity, you let go. Your inner coach reminds you to trust your own ability. You don't need confirmation from others.

Option A. The lawnmower won't be ready for two weeks. That won't do. You need it now—the grass is halfway up to the fence. So you vent your frustration at the shaken clerk. He tells you, "The shop is backed up." You keep picking at him. After this exchange the clerk is tense, and so are you.

Option B. The lawnmower won't be ready for two weeks. This is not great news. But you accept the situation and see what can be done. Can they lend you a mower? If not, can they rent you one? The clerk is helpful. You appreciate this and chat with him in a friendly way. When you leave, he feels good and so do you.

Option A. It's raining. You don't want more rain. Hourly, you shake your fist at the radio blaring out its offensive weather report. "These bloody people don't know..." You're in a bad mood all day like a bear with a thorn in its paw. You have a terrible day and so does everyone around you.

Option B. It's raining. "Oh well! Let's make the best of it," your resilient coach encourages. You put on your mackintosh and sou'wester and tromp around in the wet. You come in for a hot cup of tea, sit by the fire, munch muffins and devour a great book. You feel great all day. And so does everyone around you.

This is how we choose, in any given moment, that sweet slice of orange or that bitter lemon. Such a little thing. Such a world of difference.

On another level, our inner critic can get in the way of our ability to make positive changes, such as modifying destructive, outgrown or unwanted habits.

Are You Ready to Change?

Trying to change too much, too fast, when you're not really committed to it, can backfire... as so many people discover somewhere between January 2nd and about mid-March.

It's a familiar pattern. Come December 31st, you stub out your last cigarette, gulp down your last scotch, and indulge yourself with your absolutely last fried-egg-and-bacon sandwich. That's it, you say. And starting tomorrow, you will jog every day.

The critic takes charge, dictating the list of do's and don'ts. You know the rules. It's very straightforward: just do all the things that you usually avoid, and don't do any of the things that you usually crave. Your friends remind you they have heard this before. "I know, I know," you say, "but this time I'm *really* going to do it." Yet, you are still haunted by a nagging doubt. Why should this time be any different? Well, it just *will* be.

At first, it goes well. You do those quickie sit-ups, you put less mayonnaise on your sandwich or you stop smoking for a few weeks, but gradually your jogging shoes spend more and more time in your closet. Your rebellious side asserts its will, coaxing you with "I'm so tired. I can't go for my run today. I need something sweet for a pick-me-up. It's good to be good to yourself. Right?"

Then your critic scolds like an angry parent: "What's wrong with you? Haven't you any will-power?" The tug of war between the strict "good" side of yourself and the indulgent "bad" side can rage in a lifelong battle. The battle ground may vary, from losing weight or quitting smoking, to getting more fit or getting more organized.

Try taking a fresh approach. Try to be more aware of the emotional needs, insecurities and fears that dictate your behaviour. Accept that entrenched forces are more powerful than new ones, so change takes time. Here's another opportunity for patience.

Step back from the battle. Negotiate a cease-fire. See that you may have been brought up to believe you can get whatever you want. Right now. (Delay gratification? No way. I want it now!)

Get some perspective. You may not have learned that worthwhile things require effort. There can be pleasure in exertion and freedom in discipline. Saying no to "treats" is a strategy that you'll soon regret and is not a threat to your independence—it's a sign of being free.

The irony is that well-disciplined people whom we may regard as restricted are not as enslaved as those who indulge themselves and who can't resist temptation.

Upon reflection, come face to face with what is really going on. When you go overboard are you bored? Lonely? Restless? Angry? Frustrated? Dissatisfied?

There's no need to navel-gaze too deeply, but when you address these issues directly, you can begin to release the stranglehold of habitual patterns.

A more enlightened resolution is to make friends—with yourself, with your laziness, with your indulgence, with exertion, with discipline.

Genuine discipline is not a denial of our independence; it is freedom from laziness.

Discover the relief of being free of extremes. This is not a licence for indulging, but a key to genuine enjoyment. Savour the pleasure of moderation.

Stages of Change

Ongoing progress is more than a question of willpower. Habits are easier to break when we have developed our awareness and insight. And it's important to realize that change is a process that goes through several stages, and not necessarily in order.

Initially, you feel inspired. After a while you feel bored. Then you abandon the whole thing as a lost cause. And you feel guilty. You've failed yet again. Obviously this is beyond you.

A fresh approach is to see and accept that taking two steps forward and one step back is natural. It is expected. And progress is still being made. So when you have a "set-back," it is only another hurdle to jump. Don't be discouraged. Learn from these hurdles. Keep going. Keep transforming that spoiler critic into the go-get-'em coach.

STEP 9

Balance Your Mind, Body and Spirit

We generally interpret the world so heavily in terms of good and bad, happy and sad, nice and not nice that the world doesn't get a chance to speak for itself. [With meditation practice] we're beginning to get at this fresh way of looking when we're not caught in our hope and fear. We become mindful, awake, and gentle... The world opens up and suddenly we're there for what's happening.

Pema Chödrön
Start Where You Are

Do you ever feel that you're still preparing for life? Still working on getting things right? Getting yourself right?

While the rehearsals continue, time has a way of moving forward. One day drifts into another like colours blending together on distant hills. Months slip by before we know it, and they fade into the collage of our memories.

Feeling trapped, without options, may be one reason we don't examine if we are wasting this precious life. Coming face to face with how things are turning out, with how *we* are turning out, may be unappealing. So we keep very busy. Forging ahead, at a breakneck pace, we are consumed with just getting through each day—there is little time or energy left over for reflection.

Even when things fall apart, we want to leap abruptly into action. My job is too demanding; I'd better go on stress leave and then look for another. My head is hurting; I'd better take a painkiller. My relationship is no longer satisfying; I'd better find another. As most of us know, this approach can continue, fruitlessly, for most of our lives.

How do we slow down and become more aware of these patterns? How do we learn from them and move forward? How do we truly connect with our lives? How do we move from preparing for life to living each moment more fully?

One approach is learning how to tame the mind. Ah, the mind. This wondrous system is the treasure of our species. Controversy continues, however, about the nature of mind: is it restricted to the brain lodged in our skull. Or does it extend beyond the brain?

The brain is an intricate miracle, but some wonder if there's more to mind. New physicists, old philosophers and many ancient traditions would have us believe that there is a larger mind—a mind-energy permeating everything. That we and all phenomena are part of a vast energy system, and that nothing is permanent or solid.

Whatever and wherever the mind is, its state dictates our experience. If our mind is speedy, that is how we conduct our lives. The wildness of our thoughts and the chaos of our emotions seem to have control over us; this runaway horse takes us wherever it wants. We feel out of control because we are. The horse is riding *us*.

We experience emotional upheavals. Aggression leads us to be too forceful with our opinions. Or we come on too strong with our need for approval or our need to win. We pull back, close off and turn inward in an attempt to ignore. These habitual patterns keep us from connecting with ourselves and with each other.

We also experience the chaotic mind as discursive mental chatter. (I once heard this chatter described as being the neighbour's radio blaring on and on.) When the mind is a jumble of thoughts, there is little room for clarity or creativity.

Remember, the nervous system responds to thoughts, and the body cannot tell the difference between a real threat and an imagined threat. As you may recall, the nervous system gears up automatically when we're steaming about a perceived injustice, as if we were actually being attacked. So taking charge of the untamed mind is also taking charge of untamed stress.

Missing the Moment

The speedy mind is also unfocused. We look as if we're here—walking down the street or sitting in the meeting, but we're actually far away. Thinking. Planning. Daydreaming. We're in a fog.

Not being mindful is not paying attention. Not taking care. Not being present. Your body might be here chopping carrots, but your mind is far away. This is how we cut ourselves with the knife. How we miss the moment. How we are not fully alive. We are sleepwalking.

Our mind takes us off on some tangent, and we shift into automatic pilot to do the things at hand, which, unfortunately, often include driving the car or listening to our staff. The eyes still work, the legs still move, but we are not fully present. And if we're constantly caught up in this, we miss most moments.

We are in such a hurry that we have to feel if our toothbrush is wet to see if we have actually brushed our teeth. We find ourselves upstairs and wonder what we came here for. We've driven a few miles from home and suddenly panic—did we turn off the coffee maker?

At lunch, we wolf down that burger, and gulp that cola, without actually tasting either. We dash across town in our car and manage not to hit anything, but what do we really *see*?

At that meeting, we tromp over our co-workers' suggestions and feelings without realizing it. When we get home, we shoot out very clever solutions to the concern of our spouse, when all he or she wanted was to be heard. Our children ask us to come and see what they've done that day, and we blurt out that we'll see it later, not realizing the hurt this causes.

How often are *you* running on autopilot?

And when we are not mindful of our body, we ignore its attempts to alert us to its needs, to potential danger. Foolishly, we try to obliterate the warnings, which we call symptoms. And a lack of insight prevents us from putting the pieces of our health puzzle together.

We override our body's pleas for rest, for sleep, for water, even for a trip to the bathroom. We feel disconnected from our body and fail to experience the simple pleasures of this splendid human existence. Vivid colours. Sweet sounds. Fragrant smells. Delicate tastes. Rich textures. In the haze of our distracted mind, we miss connecting with our sense perceptions. When our mind and body are not synchronized, we become off-centre. And when we are not centred, nothing works very well.

A lack of mindfulness also affects our speech, and we fall into the unhealthy Type A speech patterns: talking too quickly, speaking too much, dominating the space. We slander, we gossip, we criticize, we're deceptive, we disparage others, and we blather on and on with stories that serve only to enhance our accomplishments. We don't take a genuine interest in others. We don't ask questions, and if we did we wouldn't bother to listen to the answers. This is self-absorption, which lacks awareness and sensitivity.

What is this "moment" stuff, anyway? It is what's happening right now. Not what happened in 1956, last week or even five minutes ago. It's the situation right in front of us. If you reflect on this, you will see that neither the past nor the future truly exists.

I work with a cardiologist—a Type A extraordinaire. His assembly-line life would exhaust most, but he seems to breeze through it. His accomplishments include the ability to focus in each moment. When he is listening to a patient, writing a report or playing golf, he is completely there.

Our inability to stay focused can be hazardous if we're carpenters or fatal if we are pilots.

The untamed mind is flabby and cannot direct itself in a specific direction or hold its attention to any one thing. (The opposite, a rigid mind, has great resistance to letting go, to allowing, to being flexible and to adapting to change.)

An untamed mind also contributes to our inability to let bygones be bygones, and this inability disrupts our peace of mind. We chew on our resentments. We build them into stories. We make them solid. They stay with us until they make us sick. So how do we learn to let go? How do we tame our mind for greater mindfulness and insight?

Taming the Mind

Think of the mind as a large lake. First, we want to become more aware of the turbulent waters of our thoughts. We need to tune into how the mind operates, instead of rushing to change it. There's not much use attempting to tame our minds on the fly. We need to take the time to sit quietly by ourselves and watch the mind. This is why we meditate. Meditation is nothing esoteric or weird. It's simply sitting quietly, calming the mind and "letting some space happen" in between our thoughts.

This may seem like a supreme waste of time, but it is the very heart of transforming ourselves into healthy Type A's.

When the mind is focused, our day-to-day experience is very different. Mental chatter subsides, opening up a fresh opportunity to connect with our natural state of mind and with things as they truly are. Emotional energy is expressed in a more positive way. Attention is now able to rest in the moment. Colours are more vivid. Sounds, more sweet. Time seems to stand still. This is what author Aldous Huxley referred to as "this timeless moment."

These moments are gaps when the mind is quiet. No, this is not being spaced out. It is more like being "spaced in." Being right here. Being fully present and awake. Our sharp edges and defences soften. We move out of the haze of a fabricated world toward greater clarity and see the world as it is. By *fabricated*, I mean a world of our making on which we project our interpretation of how things are, and in which we manipulate people and situations instead of letting them be as they are. Habitually, we try to grasp and cling to what we think will bring us pleasure, and to avoid what we thing will bring us pain. This ongoing need for control causes a plethora of problems and takes a tremendous amount of energy, and we often get it wrong.

Practising being mindful can illuminate these tendencies, help us let go, and truly see things as they are—and let them be as they are. This brings a feeling of freedom and expansiveness.

Does this mean, you ask, I could sit here at this meeting and not try to pressure everyone to see that my way is the best? I could let them have their views? And let them express their views without trouncing them? Not criticize? Not even judge? What if they don't see that we must do it my way? Wouldn't that be a terrible waste because my way is the best way?

Ah, yes, we have such confidence. But even if our way is the best one, we will still have a negative effect if we try to push it on others, if we don't listen to them and if we attempt to manoeuvre to reach our goal. If ours is the best way, we could trust that eventually the majority will come to see that. And it's so much better if the group comes to see this themselves, rather than having it stuck down their throats as we rush to get on to the next thing.

A more tamed mind balances our style—Type A or Type B. Instead of being the dictatorial bulldozer, we can become the enlightened leader. We can ask questions that help others see the wisdom of our way. We can ask them to follow their ideas through so we can all see the outcome. We can set out the facts without finding fault. And who knows, if we let go of our fixed ideas and sit back and listen, we might learn something new, and an even better plan may emerge. And we have maintained the harmony of our group. Everyone's energy is no longer zapped by meetings; once others have input into this non-judgemental process, their creative juices flow and they become recharged.

But if we become coaching leaders, can we still be go-getters? Yes, of course, but with a difference. We're now more enlightened go-getters who see the value in getting things done *and* working well with others. This approach allows us to achieve even greater success in the outside world and inside, with how we feel about ourselves. This is part of the good news! We don't have to give up our go-getter style; we just need to transform it.

In this way, we feel more grounded. More connected—with ourselves and with what is happening around us. We still have our preferences, but we ease up on manipulating others into doing it our way. Surges of energy spring forth from an untapped storehouse when we ease the grip of the need to control. Everything becomes so much more workable. We tune in to, and go with, the flow of energy that happens around us all the time. The dark cloud of conflict that used to surround our group vanishes. It's as if we stepped outside of a musty cocoon into the fresh air.

Mindfulness on the Move

Mindfulness is focusing on the task at hand. Being attentive. Taking care. It is noticing your friend is sad and withdrawn before you blather on too long about your great news. It is seeing that a person needs help opening a heavy door. It is being aware of those habitual patterns of finding fault. It is waking up.

Some would say waking up to our genuine nature of wisdom and compassion and seeing the world with clarity are the most important tasks we have in this uncertain journey called life. Yet these tasks often fall to the bottom of "to do" lists, if they're there at all.

It's important to see that we create our lives from moment to moment, like sculptors working and reworking lumps of clay. And we can turn our lives around at any age, in any moment. Mindfulness is the crucial tool.

Here is an example of how mindfulness can enhance our daily life.

You're making dinner for a family gathering. What is going though your mind? "I don't have time for this. How come my sister never has the whole family over? Why does it have to be me all the time . . . She counts on me to do everything."

Your mind is full of resentment. Your body is full of stress. As one of the children attempts to help out, you bark, "No, don't do it that way. It goes like this." Your mate is more interested in completing that special little project. Further resentment. "Can't you see that I need some help with this?"

By the time the others arrive, you're wound up in a knot and cranky. The ensuing family routines wear you down further. Why does your mother insist on pulling your hair off your forehead as if you were still a child? Why does your father insist on yakking mindlessly about the weather? When the last dish is done, you mutter that you hope it will be a long time before you have to do this again. You fall into bed, still bickering with your mate.

It could have gone differently. What if you had gathered your household together for a meeting? In our family we called them "O groups," which was an army term for a group that received orders. But they were fun. My dad, Patrick, and my mum, Anne, would tell us that we were having a special gathering. We'd all join in to make a list of the things that needed to be done, then choose which ones we'd do. Each one of us took responsibility for our jobs, and we were proud when we did them well. Neither of my parents took on the heavy-handed roll of the drill sergeant. Sometimes they had to prod us to finish a job, but this was done with kindness and encouragement. Each one of us was made to feel an essential part of the team.

My parents were effective coaches because they were supportive and caring. The stability and insight that mindfulness provides enable us to be more kind; we can see beyond someone's irritating behaviour into their heart. When your mother comes toward you with her hands poised to fix your hair, see the caring and need that motivate her. Much of her identity is tied up with her role as a caretaker. It may be hard for her to let go of that role. You might say something, gently. "Mum, I know you always liked my hair off my face, but I wear it this way now." She may or may not hear you. Accept this. Let go.

You might try this with your dad, as well. Instead of focusing on your irritation at his tendency to dominate the conversation with trivial things, look deeper. What is he feeling inside? What keeps him from expressing his feelings? Years of conditioning? Layers of stuff he doesn't want to face? An awkwardness with intimacy? When he greets you or says goodbye, he may pat or wallop you on the back, rather than give you a warm hug. But the love is there. See this. Accept this. Let go.

Try to see the dynamics of your family and appreciate them for who they are. This will ease your irritation and make your time together meaningful. This life is uncertain, and you never know when you will all be together again.

In my family we knew when it was the last time. My dear old dad was dying. My younger brother had flown in to see him for the last time. We all chipped in to make the dinner; there was no need for an O group this time. My sister-in-law and I set a beautiful table outside on the lawn with a white linen cloth and the good china. Mum gathered roses from the garden. My two brothers cooked a delicious meal.

Dad sat there in his dressing gown, his once large frame so thin now. But his eyes were still so bright and so full of love. We toasted him and told him what a wonderful father he had always been, and that we didn't want to let him go, but with sad hearts we saw that he was ready. We told him we would always love each other and always be connected. All of us felt so raw and so awake. Dad died two weeks later.

My parents had once joked that they were like an outboard motor tied to an anchor. Patrick, the outboard, was a Type A and gave the family lots of direction, inspiration and love. Anne, the anchor, is a Type B and still gives the family lots of nurturing, stability and love. For more than 50 years they delighted in each other's company, and their styles complemented each other so well.

Please appreciate your loved ones while they are here and tell them how much you care. Please do your best to be kind.

Meditation practice is helpful with all of these aspirations. The practice I am about to describe is called "mindfulness/awareness meditation." While it may be used to enhance your healing, spiritual or religious path, it is essentially a secular technique. There is nothing esoteric or religious about this contemplative practice. In the East and in the West, millions of people practise this meditation every day.

How to Meditate

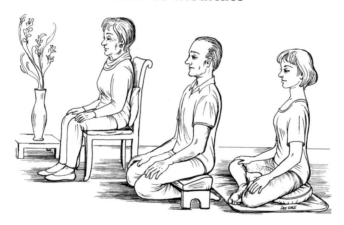

1. You sit with your legs crossed comfortably on a cushion—no points for heroic efforts to wrap your legs like a pretzel. Or you may kneel on a meditation bench or sit in a straight-backed chair. Lying on a bed or in your easy chair is not recommended.
2. Your back is upright—it's a posture of dignity and ease. Try not to let your chest cave in; lift it up a bit. This will improve your breathing and wakefulness.

3. Your head is upright, with your chin tucked in very slightly. Your neck and shoulders are relaxed. Your arms hang down straight from your shoulders, and your hands rest lightly, palms down, on top of your thighs.

4. Your eyes are open. (Why eyes open? Because in this type of meditation the focus is on connecting with our innate awareness and working at being fully present. Also, keeping your eyes open reduces daydreaming or sleepiness.)

   Your eyes are open and you look out and down, six to eight feet in front of you; your gaze is relaxed—not too tight a focus, and not too loose.

5. Your jaw is relaxed. Your mouth is slightly open. You breathe normally, in through your nose, and out through your nose and/or mouth.

6. Your attention follows the movement of your breath. Your breath comes in and out, like the movement of a swinging gate. Your breathing is your touchstone, particularly the out-breath.

So what do you do next? You sit and watch your thoughts. You get to know how your mind works.

No need to say any mantras. No need to count your breaths. In this technique you just focus on your breathing.

Thoughts come up. Do we need to stop them? No. If we try, we're only creating more activity. Do we need to make the mind go blank? No. Let the thoughts come. Let them go. Keep coming back to the breath.

Emotions come up. Do we need to get caught up in them or ignore them? No. Just let them come and let them go. Keep coming back to the breath.

So what do you do when you're aware of the breathing? You feel the movement of the breathing. Your chest and belly move to allow the breathing to happen. You feel the air going out. You feel the air coming in. There is a *light* emphasis on the air going out—on the out-breath. You're not forcing the exhalation; there's just a light sense of air going out.

You do this for a few breaths, and then you realize that your mind has shifted and is not focused on your breath. You are compiling a list of all the things that need to be done. Let these thoughts go, and go back to your breath.

After a few more breaths, you suddenly realize that your mind has wondered over to the office, and you're sorting out that deal. Back to the out-breath.

This is the practice: "being with the breath" and when you realize you are caught up in your thoughts, coming back. Over and over again, gently bring yourself back to the out-breath. To the moment.

No need to give your old critic free rein to find fault with your ability to do this ("You can't even be with a few breaths before your mind flies away!"). Those remarks are just thoughts. Let them go, and come back to the breath. No need to listen to the critic's mocking, "Why don't you get up and get something *useful* done. This is a waste of time!" Just thoughts. Let them go, and come back to the out-breath.

Should you get up and scream at your neighbour to keep her darn dog quiet because it's so distracting? No. This practice is not about ignoring or zoning out; it's about developing a way to work with things as they are. Try to work with your irritation. But if the process becomes too difficult, get up and close the window.

You are *not* trying to achieve a spiritual state of mind. Such striving creates more mental activity. To the contrary, you're trying to let go of your habitual, goal-setting mind and uncover your inherent wakefulness—a state of mind that is the free of confusion and suffering.

Some forms of meditation are geared toward "getting high" and fashioning oneself into a "spiritual" person, but the approach of mindfulness/awareness meditation is different. You're simply being quiet to calm the wildness of the mind. You are honing the mind to see patterns more clearly and to break through them—this is what is meant by *personal growth*.

You are connecting with things as they are, not as you want them to be. This practice is about being less controlling and becoming more down to earth; it's *not* about becoming ethereal.

(Remember, you are not trying to change your state of mind; you're just getting to know it better.) Thoughts and emotions are all over the map. Like weather passing overhead, your mind is cloudy one minute and clear the next, with strong winds of frustration, dark clouds of anger, fiery red sky of passion, green sky of envy. Nothing much is changing outside. You're still sitting there in your room, but your experience changes.

At some point it will dawn on you that you are creating the tone of your experience; you are creating the dramas, difficulties and limitations. You see that you've created and maintained all of these obstacles with your thoughts; these thoughts disturb your innate equanimity.

This is good news. If you are creating these thoughts and emotions, then you have the power to dissolve them. But first, just observe them. No need to analyze. No need to chastise. With more meditation practice, you will tire of these stories and the tapes will wear thin.

When you see that you have been creating this limited thinking and you can let these thoughts go, you discover the key to unlocking your potential. The practice of mindfulness/awareness meditation is the best tool I know for a life-changing transformation. It works at the very basis of our being and changes us from the ground up.

With practice, you get glimpses of the mind as it truly is—clear and calm. (This is not a belief I'm trying to impose upon you. This is an invitation to experience the intrinsic nature of the mind.)

So what would you do with a clear and calm mind? Everything. Nothing. Each action is done with just what is needed. There's a grace and economy of effort. You pour a cup of tea, and you're aware of what you're doing. It is done beautifully, but it's no big deal. No need to congratulate yourself, "Wow, can I pour one mean cup of tea!" You just do it.

Nothing more is needed. Nothing less.

There's no need to get on your case about wasted energy and about fretting over things you can't change or ignoring things you could. You are doing the best you can at the time; but now move forward. (Softening; becoming less critical and more aware is the path.) It is vital to combine your increasing awareness with increasing compassion.

How Long to Meditate?
You might start with 15 or 20 minutes at a time. Then work up to 30 minutes. Decide the time first so you can settle in: don't watch the clock. It is good to practise for longer periods when you have more time.

Where To Meditate?
In a quiet place. Create a restful, uplifted corner of beauty in your house. A place that makes you feel more at ease. You can have a flower arrangement or a picture or a candle—not to stare at—just to brighten the space. It's your sacred corner.

When To Meditate?
In the morning before you leap into your day. At your lunch break. (If you have an office and if it has a door, shut the door and hold your calls for 15 minutes. Otherwise just find any quiet place.) After work and in the evening are also good times.

Does Meditation Reduce Stress?

Yes. Your blood pressure may come down, your muscles may relax and your immune system may grow stronger; however, reducing stress is more of a by-product than a goal. In fact, the focus of this meditation is to lessen the Type A obsession with striving and always speeding off to the next thing. This practice works with these tendencies by slowing down and taming the mind. You learn to let go of thoughts and come back to the breath, over and over again. With this discipline, your attention is sharpened and becomes focused. You may still have lots of plates spinning, but you will be able to devote 100 percent of your attention to the task at hand. Then you clear your mind, re-focus and move on to dealing with the next plate, devoting 100 percent of your attention to that. This is the highest level of efficiency. This is transcending the scattered mind and realizing the focused mind. This is the key to the Plate Game.

Resistance may come up. In meditation practice, you face yourself and your life directly. You may find yourself suddenly drawn to less threatening projects such as fixing the back stairs or cleaning out the fridge. That's okay. Acknowledge this reluctance and work with it in your meditation practice. I call this "bringing everything to the path."

When you bring yourself to sit down and meditate, initially you may feel quite agitated. Your adrenalin is still high; if you sit through this, your body will settle as your system gears down. This may lead to the other extreme—boredom. Up pops your "don't just sit there, do something" script. Acknowledge the voice. Let it go. Just sit through this.

It's good to let yourself get bored; it means you're cooling down. You hate being bored, I know, but look where all that constant busyness gets you. You've been tearing about for years and getting more and more tired and less and less fulfilled. Try settling in, to calm the mind and see what happens.

Cooling down from a state of agitated, hot boredom is progress. No longer champing at the bit, you will begin to see gaps in the thickets of your thoughts. (Remember, we're not trying to stop our thoughts; we're acknowledging them, letting them go and coming back to the breath.) Then it finally happens. Your meditation pays off. "This is what is meant by *enlightenment*," you exclaim as your mind expands. You feel vast and at one with everything. There's a flash of energy, a feeling of joy and peacefulness. These experiences come and go. This "high" is *not* enlightenment. Just sit through it.

Agitation, boredom, bliss—let them come, let them go. Good thoughts, bad thoughts. Happy thoughts, sad thoughts. Let them come. Let them go. It's all the play of the mind.

How do you know when you're making progress in your meditation? A great meditation master was asked this question, and he replied quietly, "You become more kind."

Meditation and Our Scripts

Pema Chödrön, a meditation teacher and author, reminds us in her book *When Things Fall Apart* (Shambhala),

> Maybe the most important teaching is to lighten up and relax . . . to remember that what we're doing is unlocking a softness that is in us and letting it spread. We're letting that softness blur the sharp corners of self-criticism and complaint.

Meditation is very helpful in transforming the scripts formed in early life. (Remember these old tapes are just our minds nattering away.) These scolding, criticizing, blaming, interrogating thoughts sound like a parent or old teacher. By not heeding them, by letting them go, you undermine their power. And when your mind is more focused, you can reframe them; this is called "rescripting."

With a tamed mind you can shift your attitude and inner dialogue into a more positive direction, easing the harshness directed at yourself and at others.

Marie is a perfect example of this. She was always hard on herself; even when something she did went very well, she wouldn't feel nourished. It was never enough. She questioned her worth. She was quick to criticize and slow to praise—a pattern she learned as a child. With meditation, this harshness eased. Marie softened. Her self-talk changed. She was able to make a conscious effort to be more kind to herself and to others.

When Marie overheard her staff complaining about her, she was angry and hurt. Then she turned this anger on herself. "What's wrong with me? Why can't I get along better with others?" These thoughts could have mushroomed into the same old story: the staff complaining about her coming on too strong, being too masculine. She has learned to boycott that story. With meditation, she became more aware as she was *about* to jump in and take over the situation, and she was able to choose if that was the best thing to do. If not, she was able to step back and let go.

Being an impatient Type A, Marie had expected results right away. I was able to convince her that these habitual patterns had been with her for a lifetime and that, eventually negative tapes wear thin and lose their hold.

Jeremy Hayward, Ph.D., depicts this process in his remarkable book (written with his wife, Karen Hayward) *Sacred World: The Shambhala Way to Gentleness, Bravery and Power* (Shambhala):

> At some point in life, the habits that make up our cocoon were help-ful to us and protected us. Later, these same habits come to prevent us from living responsively, from opening to new possibilities. The cocoon falls away when you see it in contrast to the freshness of a moment of basic goodness, much as you may realize the air in a room is stale only when someone opens the window to let in a fresh breeze.

By stepping out of her cocoon, Marie has transformed. Some people still react to her in the same old way, being cocooned themselves, but with time most notice she has changed. When the office group was trying to decide where to go for lunch, Marie sat back and let the others decide. When her assistant told the group an anecdote, Marie did not feel compelled to top it with a funnier one. When a man she was dating hesitated, revealing a moment of insecurity, she did not write him off as weak. Marie had, indeed, changed.

Aaron also found that meditation gave him a new way to work with his mind and emotions. Achieving his goals had provided only fleeting pleasure. He was always seeking what he could not find. He was always planning, in hopes that this new destination would finally bring ease.

Many Type A's are constantly planning. Planning the next career move. Planning the next purchase. Planning the next holiday. Then we'll fill that gaping hole inside of us and feel complete. But do we feel complete? And even when the big holiday happens, do we really enjoy each moment?

Unhealthy Type A's excel at this hurry up, let's-move-on-to-the-next-thing syndrome. You've just been to the next big attraction listed in the guidebook. The map is spread on the coffee shop table. "Let's see, we're here now and if we leave in ten minutes and drive at 100 kilometres an hour, we'll be over here by tonight."

You no sooner arrive at that destination, then out comes the map. "Okay, now we're here. And if we leave right after breakfast, by lunch-time we'll be..." Are we having fun, yet? Are we ever going to be at our destination?

Insight arises from the mindfulness of meditation. We see the futility of all this scurrying around, of never being nurtured by the moment. We see that our fixation on destination has prevented us from enjoying the journey. We see the nature of that hole we feel inside and what will actually take that hollow feeling away.

We have been seeking outside what we can really find only within. When you have developed inner contentment, you can be happy just about anywhere, in just about any situation. This is unconditional happiness.

A Rousing Meditation Practice

We have discussed the taming mindfulness/awareness meditation practice; now I'd like to offer you this rousing one. Remember our dashboard and the fuel gauge? Well, this is a way to refuel by rousing our *chi*—our inner energy—and gathering the natural *chi* around us. To understand this, you need a deeper understanding of *chi*. According to Dr. Hong Zhu,

> Chi is vital energy, the energy of nature and life—in the body we call this energy the life force. We have two types of vital force *chi*: the first we get from our parents and with which we are born. The second we get from our environment—from the food we eat, the air we breathe, how we live. This is why lifestyle and attitude are so important in our well-being.
>
> This vital energy takes many forms; material *chi* maintains life; functional *chi* maintains the function of the organs; nutrient *chi* is connected with the digestive system; and defensive *chi* is connected with the immune system. When this *chi* energy of the body is blocked, problems, such as pain and illness, fatigue and depression, arise. This rousing *chi* practice, called *chi kung*, and doing Tai Chi are very helpful as they increase the circulation of the *chi* and the blood and improve the functions of all the organs of the body.

I have developed a practice to rouse *chi*. You can do this while sitting in your meditation posture or sitting at your desk. This is refuelling on the go.

1. Breathe and gear down.
2. Settle down and focus your mind the way you learned in mindfulness/awareness meditation.

3. Visualize your energy gauge. Where is your energy level? Breathe in with slow, deep breaths, and feel the energy in each breath raise the level of your gauge. Feel as if you're rousing the vital energy lying dormant in your system. It is there; you just need to waken it. And feel as if you can unblock the vital energy that is stuck in various spots where you feel pain or tightness. Visualize a stagnant pool of water beginning to flow freely as a river.
4. Breathing slowly and deeply, inhale and exhale with a gentle rhythm. Feel as if you're magnetizing the vital energy of the universe around you. It is there; you just need to gather it.
5. Visualize your energy gauge again. See the level rising as your system recharges. Feel the warmth of the energy.
6. Conclude this practice with a few moments of mindfulness/awareness meditation.

Al Huang, an innovative t'ai chi teacher, furthers our understanding of rousing *chi* in his book *Embrace Tiger, Return to Mountain.* (Real People Press).

> Energy is a confusing term. I try to make it clear that it is not nervous tension. It is subtle and powerful, and circulates continuously in one's mental/physical self. Acupuncture's meridians show the paths of this *chi* energy. In practicing T'ai Chi or Chi Kung, what one senses is the circular path of the *chi*... Beginners can only imagine it, and feel it fragmentedly. After long years of practice, it becomes very obvious. Energy is open, free-moving, unburdened, basically undefinable. It is life-force unforced, which then becomes forceful and powerful.

T'ai Chi

There is sitting meditation, and there is moving meditation such as yoga and t'ai chi. T'ai chi looks like a dance in slow motion. Yet it's much more: it's a powerful practice for those who want to gain mental alertness and physical relaxation. It's a gentle exercise for those who want to keep limber and healthy. This is an ancient system of developing the mind and body based on martial arts and has been practised for more than 2,500 years.

People of all ages can benefit from this gentle yet strengthening set of exercises. Millions of people enjoy the benefits well into their nineties. My husband, Charles Blackhall, who teaches t'ai chi and who coordinates Elderhostel here in Victoria—educational travel programs for people over 55—details the benefits:

Many elders have pain and stiffness in the shoulder, wrist, hip, knee and ankle joints. T'ai Chi works directly on these joints by continually engaging them in the subtle, flowing movements. This is of great benefit because it relaxes the body and improves balance and co-ordination. This is joining body and mind. My students tell me they have more energy, sleep better and many health problems decrease. They are more active and have less pain, and more assurance and grace. It gives them more flexibility, strength and energy. This is also very good for aging baby boomers like myself to prevent joint and stiffness from developing. T'ai Chi keeps one young.

I also practise t'ai chi. I took my first class on a beach on Cortes Island, at Cold Mountain Institute (now Hollyhock) in the early seventies. I find t'ai chi relaxing and energizing. It's also useful for focusing the mind by slowing us down and allowing us to be in the present. If an impatient go-getter like myself can gear down long enough to learn this, so can you. It's a bit tor-turous at first, it's *so* slow. But I came to appreciate the gentle pace. (I even studied Japanese tea ceremony. Now *that* could be the ultimate Type A torture—it takes a good half hour to make the darn tea. But I grew to love the gentle beauty of the prescribed movements. Such mindfulness is required; it's a great way to synchronize the body and mind.)

T'ai chi allows me to be more aware of when I'm centred and when I'm not. This is very helpful for Type A's. As you may know, we have a tendency to get off-centre by leaning out over our feet in our habitual rushing around. With t'ai chi, many of the ways to find a balance that we have talked about, such as occasionally stepping back and letting others take the lead, come more easily. So t'ai chi can help us balance our energy and our style.

Yoga

Yoga is another discipline that can be a great asset to Type A's. I have prac-tised it, on and off, over the past 25 years and highly recommend it. Anne D. Forester, Ph.D., a yoga teacher and educational consultant, has been practising and teaching yoga for more than 30 years. She studied with the yoga team that works with the remarkable physician Dean Ornish, M.D., who has documented the reversal of heart disease with yoga and meditation.

Yoga, as we practise it here in the west, is predominantly the physi-cal work of learning poses, of holding them, becoming still, and developing both stamina and flexibility. But yoga is actually the science of the mind. Its physical component, hatha yoga, was created to help still the mind, purify the body, and help us connect with our spirit. It is this larger purpose that suits it so ideally for turning lives of physical and emotional stress toward healing and calm.

By combining mind, body and spirit, yoga brings mindfulness to what could so easily be just another form of physical exercise. As you learn to use gentle breathing, paying close attention to the life force we rarely take time to observe, the entire metabolism of your body begins to slow down. Slow, deep breaths drawn in with awareness calm the body as well as the mind. The oxygen nourishes the brain and each exhalation encourages the muscles to let go, to release. Flexibility returns to the joints and the spinal column, not by the effort of stretching, but by the ability to release.

Yoga works gently, but at a deep level. The beauty of this ancient practice is that it extends so easily into our everyday life. The benefits extend far beyond the hour spent in class. Many of my students tell me that they are learning to listen to that inner voice that prompts them to breathe slowly and deeply, to let go of tight shoulders, to move the spine into a more up-right position. They come to yoga for relaxation and greater flexibility and find that its practice relieves their insomnia, reduces high blood pressure, calms a racing heart that produces angina, and releases stiff shoulders and necks.

Yoga sets no limit of age or physical ability. Young children love to work with the animal poses of rearing up like a cobra, stretching like a dog, or arching like a cat. Teen-agers have told me of the stress relief they find in yoga. At the other end of the spectrum, no matter how old or physically limited a student may be, the use of breath brings awareness and release to muscles, joints and emotional tensions.

So, how to select a class? Iyengar, Integrated and Kripalu Yoga are different styles of teaching. Iyengar is quite rigorous and physically demanding. Integrated incorporates more of the spiritual aspects and offers more relaxation. Kripalu Yoga generally moves through a fixed sequence of postures. The key component is sometimes not so much the style of the yoga, but the personality and style of the teacher. As you observe or participate, ask yourself "what qualities am I after, and does this teacher exude them?" Note also how your body responds to the work in class and be sure not to fall into a competitive mode.

These disciplines—have we come far enough that I can now use that word without your hackles going up?—are excellent antidotes to unhealthy A traits. Their very nature unravels our obsessiveness and our competitiveness. In a class, we may be tempted to strut our stuff as soon as we have something to strut, but such behaviour falls flat in this contemplative environment. Also as we gain greater confidence, we feel less need to show off.

Meditation and Healing

Meditation is moving into the mainstream. It is taught, among other places, at the University of Massachusetts Medical Centre—a major U.S. hospital. Jon Kabat-Zinn, Ph.D., is an associate professor of medicine, the founder of the Stress Reduction Clinic at the hospital, and the author of *Wherever You Go, There You Are* (Hyperion). He is internationally known for his pioneering work using mindfulness/awareness meditation to help people who are suffering from chronic pain and other medical problems.

Patients referred to him may have panic disorders, chronic back pain, high blood pressure, migraines, heart disease or cancer. While meditation itself may not shrink tumours or unclog arteries, it does help people get in touch with their minds and bodies. At the very least, the program enables people to find an inner calmness and strength that reduces their stress and helps them take care of themselves. What's more, most of the patients report that their psychological and physical symptoms show remarkable improvement over the eight-week course. And the improvements are long term. When researchers did a follow-up study of 225 chronic pain sufferers who participated in the program, 72 percent of those who answered a questionnaire reported moderate-to-great improvement in their pain—even after three years. Nearly all of those people had continued to meditate and do yoga regularly.

Dr. Kabat-Zinn and the inspiring physician Deepak Chopra, M.D., are trail-blazers who are bringing much-needed ancient wisdom to modern-day healing and helping to change conventional medicine. By integrating *ayurveda*—the ancient Indian system of healing—into modern medicine, Dr. Chopra has advanced the field of complementary medicine. In his many books, including *Ageless Body, Timeless Mind* (Harmony Books), and in his medical practice, he proposes that we are constantly creating the state of our health by our thoughts. And by changing the patterns of our thoughts, we can change our health. Dr. Chopra has taken a courageous leap from the "scientific" model, which refused to acknowledge the existence of anything that defied quantification by these scientists' instruments.

This progressive view is also expressed by Houston Smith, a professor at the University of California, Berkeley, in *Forgotten Truth* (HarperCollins).

> The triumphs of modern science went to man's head in something of the way rum does, causing him to grow loose in his logic. He came to think that what science discovers somehow casts doubt on what it does not discover; that the success it realizes in its own domain throws into question the reality of domains its devices don't touch.

This comment describes so well why many medical practitioners are skeptical about things they can't measure, can't dissect and can't even see— like *chi*—with the instruments they use. And this skepticism keeps their minds closed to ancient healing systems like acupuncture and natural medicine and even the healing power of the mind through prayer, meditation or visualization.

Charles Tart, Ph.D., is another proponent of mindfulness/awareness meditation. In his wonderful book, *Living the Mindful Life, a Handbook for Living in the Present Moment* (Shambhala), he reminds us:

> It does not take a strenuous effort to make yourself become mindful and more present. The problem is remembering to do it. We forget all the time ... Yet it is possible to learn to be mindful in our daily lives, to see more accurately and discriminatingly and so behave more appropriately toward others and toward our inner selves as well.
>
> The results cannot be fully described in mere words, but words and phrases like "freshness, attentiveness, beginner's mind, or aliveness" point in the right direction. A stale and narrow life of habit and conditioned perceptions, feelings and actions can slowly be transformed into a more caring, more effective and more intelligent life.

None of these practices are sure-fire, quick-fix remedies. They are, however, ancient disciplines that have given generations of high-powered and low-key people an effective working base for dealing with life's pressures. I have personally benefitted from this wisdom and encourage you to look into ways to balance your mind, body and spirit. Be cautious: there are lots of questionable, self-styled teachers promising results. Trust your intuition here. As we become healthier Type A's our intuition blossoms.

STEP 10

Awaken the Wisdom Within

Kindness is more important than wisdom,
and the recognition of this is the beginning of wisdom.

Theodore Isaac Rubin

Now that we have come this far together, we have reached the point where we can begin to let go of labels. We can stop analyzing the left and right brain, stop seeing the distinctions between Types A and B, and quell the inner debate between the critic and coach.

If I didn't think all these things were useful and important, I wouldn't have written all those steps! We need to be more informed and more aware at this level to build the essential foundation of wellness and energy.

Farther along in our journey, though, we are moving away from the dualism, the assessment, the analysis and the search for external solutions. Now we are at the stage of integration, wholeness and awakening the wisdom within.

With the foundation that we have established through the previous nine steps, we have developed to a stage where we can allow them to become a natural part of our daily routine.

We now see our style more clearly. We have learned to slow down, recognize our cue, breathe more effectively and gear down. We are now more patient and take things as they come. In Steps 5, 6 and 7, we became medical sleuths, seeking to clarify the root, the symptoms and the path toward effective treatment, to improve our health. We now know many practical ways to boost our batteries and refuel naturally. In Step 8, we re-visited the behavioural aspects, with a greater perspective. Easing the grip of the critic gets to the heart of many unhealthy aspects of our Type A style. The coach has become our counsellor, reminding us about all of these steps, and an ally in our personal growth.

In Step 9, we focused on essential assets in this journey. While the breathing exercises and stress techniques in Step 4 are instrumental in taking charge of our nervous system, this step is only part of the picture. It is essential to combine these techniques with Steps 8 and 9.

The practice of sitting meditation is, in my experience, the most useful method I have found in my quest for balance and awareness. Yoga and t'ai chi are also old friends. Like many people, I was skeptical about all this *chi* stuff; how can it be real if we can't see it under a microscope or even feel it in our bodies? I have come to see that I don't need to analyze, dissect and debate everything. There are some things that I can feel and sense intuitively.

As I have inched forward in my growth, I have realized that having glamorous clothes, jewellery, trips, jobs or even a glamorous mate or a loving child does not bring lasting satisfaction; that it is futile to seek happiness in external things; and that most "self-improvement" projects are also looking in the wrong direction. I see now that clarity, kindness, contentment—our basic goodness—already exist within us; they just need to be nurtured. These qualities will shine through once we quiet the mind and shed those layers of expectations, pretence and defence. This is what I mean by *awakening the wisdom within.*

After saying that we were moving beyond distinctions, I'd like to make another one. I used to think of spirituality as being inextricably tied with religion. I now know this is not the case. Seeking deeper meaning and transcendent values is not in conflict with our love of family and appreciation of the day-to-day world. We don't have to give away all our possessions and remove ourselves from commitments to family and work to find a spiritual way of being. These elements are not distractions; they make up the path and fuel for our journey.

We can have this spiritual awareness in combination with religious practice, but this connection is not essential for everyone. Developing spiritually is, for me, about becoming more fully human. Increasing our caring and compassion for others and for ourselves. It is appreciating the preciousness of this human life and of all life, and seeing the interconnectedness of everything. This book and this program are for you, and it is my sincere wish that you will find each step beneficial. Some of you will use these steps to ease your own suffering; some of you will go on to ease the suffering of others and discover what meaningful contribution you can make to this world.

There seems to be what I call a "nineties existential" crisis growing in our "successful" society. What are we here for? What is this life really all about? What do I want out of this life? And how can I get it?

Many of us have so much—not to say that we have paid for it all—and still happiness eludes us. Will having more stuff make us feel more complete? We come to see that we're facing the prospect of getting older, greyer and thicker around the middle. Will more years make us feel more satisfied?

These are spiritual questions. And seeking their answers can bring a lot of frustration or a lot of richness.

There are many enlightening books to guide us with these questions. One of the first ones I found illuminating was called *The Master Game* (Delacorte Press, now out of print) by a biochemist called Robert de Ropp. He wrote that in this life we all have stated or unstated games and goals. These exist on various levels.

The goal of the Hog in Trough Game, a lower game, was accumulation. Dedicated players joke that "those who die with the most toys win." Ha. Ha.

Another lower game is Cock on Dunghill. The goal here was self-promotion and ego-centred power.

Then, there were two more worthy games: the Science, Arts and Beauty Game, where one sought knowledge and culture, and the Householders' Game of creating a loving and harmonious family. De Ropp saw these pursuits as enriching and worthwhile.

The pinnacle was, however, the Master Game—what he called "self-realization." This is what psychologist Carl Jung called "individuation" and other disciplines call "waking up" or "enlightenment." This awakening is not cramming in as many personal development courses and videotaped personal power programs as we can afford. It is more about letting go of the self than it is about perfecting it. It is about seeing the futility of striving for and seeking fulfillment outside of ourselves.

Last summer my husband and I were camping in the Rockies. It was invigorating being in the high mountains. The air was clear. The sky was vast. One night we joined other groups in camp-fire songs. There were people from across the country—we sang Newfoundland ditties, Nova Scotia ballads, French-Canadian *chansons* and Canadian classics with equal fervour. Looking around the circle, I was struck by the sheer joy on the faces illuminated by the glow of the fire. Someone played an autoharp, the rest of us played on spoons and whatever we could use for drums. Unable to resist the beat, many of us danced around the fire. The moon was full. The night was charged with energy. You don't find this kind of fun in a big city. Divisions and the usual seemingly solid boundaries that we set up between people and between parts of the country dissolved.

The next day, we said our farewells with genuine sadness; we would probably never meet again. One fellow looked particularly sorry to see us go. He told me that he had been really touched by the camaraderie around the camp-fire.

> I haven't had that much fun since I was a kid. I'm a corporate lawyer. We work at a brutal pace. It's a very tough, dog-eat-dog world. I couldn't believe how great it felt to sing all those songs. And how close I felt to people I don't even know. A few years ago, when I was in Africa on a business trip, I heard that tribal people believe that if no one plays a drum, the drum is sleeping. Well, I've been sleeping.

He had been truly alive at that camp-fire, belting out show tunes with pizazz and dancing with abandon. (His law partners would have been in for quite a shock.) It is these experiences that contrast the soullessness of our concrete cocoons. They wake us up and open our hearts.

Alice Walker, the Pulitzer prize–winning author of *The Color Purple* (Pocket Books), is an advocate of living our lives with more heart.

> You know what hearts are for? Hearts are there to be broken, and I say that because that seems to be just what happens with hearts. I mean, mine has been broken so many times that I have lost count. But it just seems to be broken open more and more, and it just gets bigger.

Another author and long-time practitioner of mindfulness/awareness meditation, Jack Kornfield, shares his wisdom in *A Path With Heart—A Guide through the Perils and Promises of Spiritual Life* (Bantam Press):

> Even the most exalted states and the most exceptional spiritual accomplishments are unimportant if we cannot be happy in the most basic and ordinary ways, if we cannot touch one another and the life we have been given with our hearts.

The wider vision of becoming a healthy Type A is being more concerned with others and with the world around us. We may have been rather self-absorbed; we are, after all, so amusing, so bright, so confident, so every-thing. But as we progress along the path, we see that we have also been so arrogant. And we begin to discover the genuine power in being more gentle, and sensitive to the people and the world around us.

Becoming a more responsible citizen of this planet doesn't take any more time—it doesn't take any longer to toss that recyclable plastic bottle into the recycling bin than it does to toss it into the trash.

The Dalai Lama gave a talk in Victoria a few years ago on the environ-ment. He cupped his hands in his lap and said, "This blue planet is our only home. The moon and stars look wonderful in the sky, but we cannot live there. We must take good care of this, our only home."

A shift in our values, and in our actions, will not only help our "only home," it will yield great personal benefit—simplification.

It sounds easy enough. And like a worthwhile goal. However, to actually simplify our lives is quite a challenge.

By this time in our journey through life, we're pretty hemmed in: most of our income is eaten away in paying for a roof over our heads, clothes to wear, transportation and food to eat. The rest of our hard-earned money goes to taxes. So given all this, how can we simplify? Quit our job? Sell the house? Get rid of the kids?

Doesn't simplifying mean we have to work less, need less, buy less and do less? Perhaps, to some degree, but that's not the whole picture. One of the greatest challenges in taking charge is working with situations as they are—being more attuned to reality, rather than trying to buck it.

For example, when we're not happy in our job or relationship, the conventional approach is to move on. Obviously, the problem is with our impossible boss, with our impossible partner. Or is it?

After we've been through several unhappy jobs and unhappy relation-ships, we begin to see what *we* bring to the situation. What pressures are self-created? Do we expect too much of ourselves?

Simplifying may include saying no. "No, I'm sorry I am not able to take that on now." "No, I don't need to buy another outfit when my closet is crammed with so much stuff." "No, I won't step into the fray of that conflict." "No, I don't need to work myself into a tizzy over this dinner party, when a simple meal and a relaxed atmosphere will please the guests more." "No, I can't do that today. I really need some time for myself. Time to recharge."

If we have difficulty saying no, we need to look at our conditioning. Many of us were programmed at an early age: "Be nice," "Be agreeable,"

"It doesn't matter how we feel inside. Just keep smiling and just keep going." Isn't it time to let go of some of this tiresome stuff?

Now let's look at external factors. If we list our spinning plates, we realize why we're so worn down at the end of the week. Most of us are trying to do too much. But, as we said, there doesn't seem to be much choice. Or is there?

What are we doing now that we could let go of? This may include extra responsibilities in our professional and personal lives. Perhaps, it's time to let someone else take on organizing the staff social events, sitting on the parents' committee or hosting the family gatherings. Doers sometimes need to let others get more involved.

Simplifying is also about getting rid of things we don't use and reducing our needs. Maybe it's time to sort through all that stuff and have a garage sale. This creates more space in the house and some extra cash. (Alas, some of that stuff will end up at my house, as my husband is a devoted garage-saler.)

Simplifying can be a team effort. Just discussing the weight we feel upon our shoulders lessens the load. We can inspire each other to let go. We can inspire each other to rediscover the relaxation of simpler times.

Awakening Kindness

Underneath all the layers of competitiveness, aggression and self-absorption, lies our basic nature. Here, within us, is the kindness that arises when we awaken the wisdom within. Kindness doesn't need to be created, it is in us already.

When you hear the word kindness, what images arise? A tender-hearted granny pouring cups of tea? A loving parent soothing a child? Someone going out of his or her way to do another's errand?

What about a boss turning away from the computer to listen to an employee? Or stopping to ask if the staff have everything they need to do the job? Or praising an assistant for a job well done? Mother Teresa, we know, was kind. But can we be kind, in our daily lives? Even at work?

Kindness in the workplace may seem like an oxymoron, but it's a growing trend. Many progressive organizations are discovering morale and productivity increase dramatically when people are more considerate to each other. And innovative leaders are working to develop kindness and consideration in their teams. Old-style managers who may have scorned this "warm and fuzzy" approach are beginning to take notice at the results their newer-style colleagues achieve with their kinder, gentler manner.

Which boss do you remember fondly? Which teacher inspired you the most at school? Was he or she self-absorbed and easily irritated? Not likely. I bet one of the qualities that you were drawn to is kindness.

At home with our families, out with our friends, at work with our colleagues—there are so many opportunities to be kind. But it's best not to make this a big project. Genuineness is crucial; syrupy, cloying manipulative "kindness" is not. We want to give others more space, not smother them.

The heart of genuine kindness is having more concern for others and less concern for ourselves. In a conversation, for example, are you overcome by the need to tell your story, to get your point across, or can you step back and let others express theirs? Giving others some room brings greater happiness to them and to us. Being more tuned into others, and what is happening around us is essential in kindness. Awareness, as ever, is key.

Another life treasure worth nurturing is our ability to appreciate every moment.

A dear friend who was coming to visit for two weeks called to ask if she could bring her 80-year-old grandmother. "Ah, yes, of course," I replied. But I wasn't sure. Would her grandmother keep up with us or dampen our fun?

The day arrived. I went out to meet the car, with some apprehension. Suddenly, a petite woman with silvery hair leaped out from the front seat, strode over and shook my hand, "Hello, I'm Grace—the old Granny!" I was immediately struck by her sparkling blue eyes and warm smile.

In the next two weeks, Grace taught us a lot. First, I learned about stamina. She "paid the rent" for her body, as she said, with daily stretching and a brisk walk. And I do mean *brisk*.

Grace was fit and trim. She savoured fresh vegetable salads with the lip-smacking delight most of us reserve for death-by-chocolate truffles. Her quiet self-discipline was remarkable. No hardship. No fanfare. "I just feel better eating this way," she offered.

Second, I learned more about being in the moment. The world as seen through Grace's eyes was a constant source of pleasure.

"Look at that vivid blue sky!" she exclaimed, jolting me out of a daze.

"What fun to hear the children's laughter," she mused, snapping me out of my irritation at "all that racket."

We took her to a film of the ballet *Swan Lake*. The theatre seats were uncomfortable. The sound wasn't good. There were rowdy teens in front of us. I was sitting there chewing over these grievances when Grace leaned over and whispered to me, "Isn't this marvellous?"

Was she in the same place I was?

"But, Grace, aren't those kids bothering you?"

"Oh no, my dear. This musical experience will enrich their whole lives."

Grace made more friends in Victoria in two weeks than a lot of people who have spent their lives here. She admired the neighbours' delphiniums, praised the checkout woman for her cheerfulness and told the waiter how much she appreciated his attentive service.

I never heard her say a harsh thing about anyone or anything.

And there was such magic in the way she listened. When those bright eyes were focused on you, you felt so good. You would do anything for her.

Through Grace, I learned the power of appreciation.

About The Author

Kerry Crofton has a PhD in psychology and specializes in stress and wellness in the workplace. Her background includes writing a weekly newspaper column; conducting university lectures; leading a coronary prevention program; opening a clinical practice; and directing a biofeedback and stress management institute. She is currently developing a radio program.

Dr. Crofton is with the National Speakers Bureau and her keynote presentations and seminars have been well received throughout North America. She has worked with men and women in many high-stress occupations such as teaching, health care, the Armed Forces, commercial aviation and air-traffic controlling.

She lives with her husband, Charles, and son, Nigel, in Victoria, British Columbia.

For those of you wishing to visit Dr. Crofton's website, her address is:
www.pacificcoast.net/~kerry

Dr. Kerry Crofton . . . On the Platform

**One of North America's leading speakers, with a focus on
stress and wellness in the workplace.**

Dr. Kerry Crofton addresses the needs of Type A's and those who work with
them. As a self-diagnosed Healthy Type A™ personality who has learned to
maintain a balanced lifestyle through awareness and skillful action, she
speaks from both knowledge and personal experience.

Kerry has worked with hundreds of organizations, private sector companies, and many federal and provincial government departments. She provides keynote speeches, counselling and consulting throughout North
America.

For more information concerning personal appearances by
Kerry Crofton, contact:

NATIONAL SPEAKERS BUREAU
1-800-661-4110
Fax: 604-224-8906
E-Mail: speakers@nsb.com
Website: http://www.nsb.com

Order Form

Healthy Type A™: Cassette Tapes by Kerry Crofton:

- **Relax/Recharge**
- *as described in Step 4*

Side One – Belly breathing and muscle relaxation.
Side Two – Belly breathing and hand warming.

_____ (# of Relax/Recharge cassette tapes) @ $15.00   = _____

- **Mindfulness/Awareness Meditation**
- *as described in Step 9*

Side One – Instruction on how to meditate.
Side Two – A guided meditation

_____ (# of Mindfulness Meditation cassette tapes) @ $15.00 = _____

Healthy Type A™: Video:

- **Balancing Mind/Body/Spirit**
- *as described in Step 9*

Yoga stretches and relaxation with Anne Forester.
T'ai Chi/Chi Kung exercises with Charles Blackhall.
Mindfulness meditation with Kerry Crofton.

_____ (# of video tapes) @ $25.00   = _____

These prices include all taxes, shipping and handling.   Total _____

Check here if you want to receive:

_____ Free Health Letter with more information and local resources.

_____ Free catalogue from Source Books.

Source Books
24 Pittmann Cr.
Ajax, Ontario L1S 3G3
Tel: (905) 427-1051
Fax: (905) 427-6728
sourcebk@inforamp.net